What's Ahead in Education?

An Analysis of the Policies of the Obama Administration

William Hayes

ROWMAN & LITTLEFIELD EDUCATION
A division of
ROWMAN & LITTLEFIELD PUBLISHERS, INC.
Lanham • New York • Toronto • Plymouth, UK

KH

Published by Rowman & Littlefield Education
A division of Rowman & Littlefield Publishers, Inc.
A wholly owned subsidiary of The Rowman & Littlefield Publishing Group, Inc.
4501 Forbes Boulevard, Suite 200, Lanham, Maryland 20706
http://www.rowmaneducation.com

Estover Road, Plymouth PL6 7PY, United Kingdom

British Library Cataloguing in Publication Information Available

Library of Congress Cataloging-in-Publication Data

Hayes, William, 1938–
  What's ahead in education? : an analysis of the policies of the Obama administration / William Hayes.
    p. cm.
  Includes bibliographical references and index.
  ISBN 978-1-60709-679-5 (cloth : alk. paper) — ISBN 978-1-60709-680-1 (pbk. : alk. paper) — ISBN 978-1-60709-681-8 (electronic)
  1. Education and state—United States. 2. United States—Politics and government—2009– 3. Obama, Barack. I. Title.
  LC89.H395 2010
  379.73'0905—dc22
                                                          2010024674

∞™ The paper used in this publication meets the minimum requirements of American National Standard for Information Sciences—Permanence of Paper for Printed Library Materials, ANSI/NISO Z39.48-1992.

Printed in the United States of America

3/6/10

Contents

Part III The Future

Foreword

The president of the United States has often been described as the most powerful person in the world. This important individual has four or eight years to set policy and chart the course in a host of areas for the strongest nation, the most stable democracy on earth.

A president's past experience invariably shapes thoughts and attitudes on all of the issues that must be confronted during that administration. This is especially true of education, because every president has received some brand of American education. Thinking about education has been important to Americans for decades. Educational policy has been on the front burner for most presidential administrations since the end of the Second World War.

My introduction to this phenomenon was in 1985, when I was beginning a second doctoral degree as a relatively young academic administrator. I had a discipline-specific doctorate in my teaching field, but after moving into a deanship, I realized I did not have any training in educational theory or praxis. As I began this new doctoral degree program at the University of North Texas, I was confronted with the important report titled *A Nation at Risk*, completed just two years earlier in the Reagan administration by an eighteen-member panel under the leadership of David Gardner.

As I pursued this subject, I found that this was one of a series of educational studies commissioned by several presidents, beginning with the *Truman Report* in 1947 and including a report in 1956 during the Eisenhower administration by the Committee on Education beyond the High School. Perhaps the most famous was the Kennedy administration's Task Force on Education in 1960. More recently, the Spellings Commission produced *A Test of Leadership* in 2006, during the George W. Bush administration. The most famous portion of that, of course, is the No Child Left Behind legislation.

It will be very interesting to see what President Obama and his administration will do about education. In this age of globalization, with the rise of world-class universities in many parts of the world that used to be somewhat devoid of education, and with a number of countries pouring great percentages of their national resources into all levels of education, there is increasing concern that the United States is lagging.

This educational shortfall is only one area of concern for the Obama administration, but it is a fundamental one, because how our country handles education will spill over into the way we deal with all of the other major problems that we are facing.

In this study, Professor Bill Hayes, a veteran administrator in the public sector and now, for more than a decade, a college professor and researcher, examines the influences on President Obama and the problems he and his administration are confronting. History will tell us, years from now, how successful this man will be in charting a good course for our country, but Professor Hayes finds many clues to the future in his careful analysis.

Tracing the early years of Mr. Obama's own education, and then carefully documenting his short Senate career and his promises on the campaign trail, Professor Hayes is able to begin to uncover the philosophy that guides our forty-fourth president. In addition, he carefully analyzes the appointment of Secretary Duncan and the Race to the Top initiative to interpret how those factors will influence the future of our schools.

Undoubtedly, this administration will make major changes in the way education is perceived and performed in America. Professor Hayes' work helps us set the stage as we watch, in the early days of this administration, what goes on—and as we participate in this important task.

John A. Martin, ThD, PhD
President, Roberts Wesleyan College

Acknowledgments

There are a number of people to thank for helping in the preparation of this book. First and foremost is Lisa Dietz, a student assistant in the Teacher Education Division at Roberts Wesleyan College. Along with typing the entire manuscript, she has assisted in the research and the editing. Lisa has been a true partner in this project. Several other colleagues have helped with the preparation of the book. Marty Garland did an excellent job proofreading every chapter. Linda Jones, our college's director of reference and bibliographic instruction, provided many of the sources used. With this my fourteenth book for Rowman & Littlefield, I wish to express my thanks to the vice president and editorial director of the education division of Rowman & Littlefield Publishing Group, Dr. Thomas Koerner, for his confidence in me as an author and for his many valuable suggestions for my projects. Tom is a wonderful associate. Finally, as with my previous thirteen books, my wife, Nancy, has proofread every page and has offered helpful suggestions that have improved the final product. I am indebted to all of these individuals for their interest and support in the completion of this project.

Introduction

One certainly cannot predict with precision what any leader will do in regard to a specific policy issue. His or her actions will undoubtedly be affected by the social, economic, and political conditions that are present at the time any initiatives are introduced. In attempting to determine the direction of Barack Obama's policies in the field of education, what can be done is to study the president's personal experiences, his written and spoken words on the subject, and his actions in the area prior to becoming our nation's chief executive.

As President Obama assumed office, perhaps his biggest challenge in the field of education was to deal with the reauthorization of the controversial law known as No Child Left Behind. Already several years overdue for reauthorization, the thousand-plus-page law, which is currently impacting almost all schools in the nation, has generated conflict at every level in our society. Even though it is impossible to quarrel with the goal of the legislation, most educational interest groups have developed proposals for making both major and minor changes in the current law.

There are also a number of vocal critics who are more than ready to get rid of the legislation entirely. Because public education has historically been the responsibility of state and local government, there is a lack of agreement in our nation as to what role the federal government should be playing in this area. The reauthorization of No Child Left Behind is only one of the potential educational reforms that will be considered during the Obama presidency. During his political career, before becoming president, there were many clear signs as to his views on education. I will attempt to identify the major policy initiatives the president is proposing and examine the arguments surrounding each issue.

To provide the necessary background for his proposals, I will begin by looking at the president's own formal education. This will be followed by an examination of his work experiences as a community organizer, college instructor, and lawyer. His work as a member of the state legislature in Illinois and while a United States Senator will also be considered.

Additional clues to his thoughts on the subject can be found in his two best-selling books, *Dreams from My Father* and *The Audacity of Hope*. Certainly there is something to be learned by studying his comments on education during the 2008 presidential campaign. Finally, the billions of dollars allotted to the states in his economic stimulus package provide further evidence of the president's commitment to education.

The restrictions placed upon the state governments for the use of this money offer clear evidence of several of the administration's educational beliefs. In developing these programs, a major player has been the Secretary of Education, Arne Duncan. It would seem helpful to learn about the background and the previous career of this man, who is undoubtedly a trusted adviser of the president.

It is also true that by the summer of 2010, the Obama education agenda had become quite clear. There were still many details to be dealt with, and undoubtedly there were serious questions about how much support the administration would have in Congress and from powerful groups such as the teachers unions. What is clear, thus far in his presidency, is that Barack Obama does care deeply about education policy and that it will be a significant public issue in the days ahead.

For me, the experience of writing this book can be summed up by a quote attributed to journalist and author David Halbertstram. It is taken from a recent book by Richard N. Haass titled *The War of Necessity and the War of Choice*. Halbertstram described what he felt after writing one of his books by saying, "A book like this does not have a simple, preordained, linear life. A writer begins with a certainty that the subject is important, but the book has an orbital drive of its own—it takes you on its own journey, and I have learned a great deal."[1] So let us begin the journey.

NOTE

1 Richard N. Haass, *War of Necessity, War of Choice: A Memoir of Two Iraq Wars* (New York: Simon & Schuster, 2009), 16.

I

THE PREPARATION OF AN EDUCATIONAL LEADER

1

The Education of a Future President

The feelings and opinions of most people concerning a topic such as education are very likely to be impacted by the person's family and his or her own educational experiences. Barack Obama is the product of both a unique family and an unusual educational background. Both of these factors are bound to be somewhat influential in affecting any educational reform initiatives he might support as president. To better understand the man who became our national leader, perhaps the place to start is by considering his family. The product of an interracial marriage, he often refers to his own background when talking about students and schools.

There is reason to believe that the best place to begin is with a discussion of the president's father. Although he spent only a short time in direct contact with Barack Obama Sr., upon his graduation from Harvard Law School, Obama wrote a book that speaks to the impact of this man on his life. Titled *Dreams from My Father,* the book has become a best seller. In the first chapter, he described his feelings this way: "At the time of his death, my father remained a myth to me, both more and less than a man. . . . As a child I knew him only through the stories my mother and grandparents told. They all had their favorites, each one seamless, burnished smooth from repeated use."[1]

His father was a member of the Luo tribe in Kenya. Obama's paternal grandfather was a prominent member of the tribe who was a successful farmer as well as a medicine man. At the age of twenty-three, his father, Barack Obama Sr., won a scholarship to attend a university in the United States. He chose to enter the University of Hawaii in 1959 to study econometrics and graduated in three years at the top of his class. It was during his

3

undergraduate years in Hawaii that he met a "shy American girl, only 18, and they fell in love." They were quickly married and she bore him a son to whom he bequeathed his name.

When he won another scholarship, this time to pursue a doctorate at Harvard, he was unable to afford to take his young family with him. The only time Obama can actually remember his father was when he was ten years old and his father visited for a month in Hawaii.[2] The years following this visit were sometimes unhappy ones for his father. He would in his forty-six years of life have three wives, seven sons, and a daughter. In the book *The American Journey of Barack Obama*, Barack Obama Sr. is described as being "bright and gregarious" and possessing "quite a mischievous streak."[3]

Even after the divorce of his mother and father, the parents continued to correspond and Barack received occasional letters from his father. His mother was also present during the Hawaiian visit when Barack was ten years old. After earning his PhD at Harvard, the senior Obama returned to Kenya, where he worked for the Kenyan government and later for a U.S. oil company.

In his years in Kenya, he is described as being a "stubbornly principled man with a giving nature." Unfortunately, his strong opinions led him to be fired by the government, and for a time he lived in near poverty and engaged in heavy drinking. Despite these problems, those who knew him have observed similarities between the president and his father.[4]

His half sister, Auma, who knew both men, observed to a reporter from the *Guardian*: "His hand movements, his gestures, how he talks, how he sits. He's got a certain quietness about him and he sits and he concentrates like my father. He can be in a room full of people and he withdraws on his own. And we've all got the Obama hands—the fingers and everything. So it was amazing to watch that, because I was meeting him for the first time, but it felt like I knew him."[5]

By choosing to write a book titled *Dreams from My Father*, it is clear that Barack Obama was affected by the fact that he had an absentee father. Certainly this void in his life has led him to speak frequently, especially to African American men, on their duty to be role models for their children. On the other hand, the educational achievement of his father, as well as his mother, in earning a doctorate has undoubtedly impressed him.

Even as a mature adult, President Obama would still admit that it is difficult for him to fairly assess the impact of his father on his life. What he wrote in his book probably still represents his true feelings today: "He remains opaque to me, a present mass; when I mimic his gestures or turns of phrase, I know neither their origins nor their consequences, can't see how they play out over time."[6] While questioning the impact of his father, he is much clearer about the influence of his mother.

Time magazine described Stanley Ann Dunham Soetoro as a "a teen mother who later got a Ph.D. in anthropology; a white woman from the Midwest who was more comfortable in Indonesia; a natural-born mother obsessed with her work; a romantic pragmatist, if such a thing is possible."[7] Born in Kansas, she moved to Hawaii with her furniture-salesman father and her mother.[8]

After her marriage and divorce, she relocated with her son to Jakarta in Indonesia and began her study to become an anthropologist. In doing so, she wrote an eight-hundred-page doctoral dissertation on peasant blacksmithy in Java. Following this, she worked for the Ford Foundation, where she became an advocate for women and the poor. Despite the fact that she was a busy working woman, her son remembers her waking him up at 4 a.m. to teach him using correspondence courses in English.[9] The fact that both his mother and father were undoubtedly intellectuals with strong views on social issues certainly fostered in their son many of the same interests.

Her son has described his mother as a "dreamer" who could be at times "reckless" and seemed to always be "searching for something." In addition, she has been labeled by others as being very capable and fearless. As he is apparently sensitive about his father's neglect of the family, Barack Obama has also turned away from his mother's restless tendency to move about and leave others in charge of her children. Amanda Ripley, in an article published in *Time*, emphasized the complications in the life of Mrs. Obama by pointing out that at different times she was known by four different names. Both the president and his wife, Michelle, are devoted to personally raising their children.[10]

Despite the time that she spent apart from her son, Barack and other members of the family have claimed that her influence on her son has been significant. It would appear that her attitudes about people and the need to understand their differences, as well as the conviction that people can work together to solve problems, are lessons that the president may have learned from his mother. The importance of his mother in his life is illustrated by his statement that his biggest mistake "was not being at his mother's side when she died" of ovarian cancer on November 7, 1995.[11]

When Barack returned to Hawaii from Indonesia, he lived with his grandparents in a two-bedroom high-rise. His grandfather, who was always referred to as Gramps, had left the furniture business and was struggling in a new career as an insurance salesman. Despite his lack of a college education, Gramps was thrilled that with the help of his employer, his young grandson was accepted at a prestigious private high school, the Punahou Academy. On his first visit to the campus, with its tennis courts, swimming pools, and photography studios, Gramps said, "Hell, Bar . . . this isn't a school. This is heaven. You might just get me to go back to school with you."[12]

Although sometimes difficult and temperamental, there is no question that Gramps loved his grandson and encouraged him to do well in school. The individual taking the most interest in Barack's high school education was his grandmother, affectionately known as Toot. As a young girl during the Second World War, Madelyn Dunham worked on a bomber assembly line. She married Stanley Dunham and together they moved to three different states before finally settling in Hawaii. Although Toot never earned a college degree, she did take college courses and would eventually be promoted from being a secretary to become one of the first female bank vice presidents in the state of Hawaii.[13]

Even after Barack left Hawaii for college, his grandmother continued to stay in contact with him. In an interview with the president's half sister, she expressed her feeling that "from our grandmother, he gets his pragmatism, his levelheadedness, his ability to stay centered in the eye of the story, . . . his sensible, no-nonsense is inherited from her." Obama himself would say, "She's the one who taught me about hard work. . . . She's the one who put off buying a new car or a new dress for herself so that I could have a better life. She poured everything she had into me." He clearly demonstrated his love for her by suspending his presidential campaign to visit her and later to attend her funeral.[14]

The impact of his parents and grandparents was undoubtedly a factor in shaping the president's understanding of the importance of education. By word and example, they were successful in convincing him that working hard in school would open doors for him in the future. The adults in his life who were most important to him encouraged and pushed him to succeed in school. As a student, he was endowed with natural ability, but the encouragement of his parents and grandparents helped ensure that he would succeed at every level of his formal education.

Perhaps equally important is the fact that, without exception, he attended outstanding schools. Beginning with kindergarten, the future president had positive experiences as a student. Actually, his only exposure to a public school in the United States was in the kindergarten class of Ms. Sakais. He was only in this class for a couple of months before he left for Indonesia in 1967. The Department of Education in Hawaii has been unable to locate any record of attendance at school, although a picture has been discovered in which Obama is one of twenty-seven students.[15]

During his first three years in Indonesia, he attended St. Francis of Assisi Catholic School. It was a school established for wealthy Dutch aristocrats during the 1930s. His final year of schooling was in an Indonesian public school. There have been those who have claimed that this was a Muslim institution and that during his time there, he was indoctrinated in that faith.

Obama himself has denied that this was the case and a number of administrators, instructors, and classmates have supported this assertion, claiming that instruction in the school was "general" and that the student body was made up of children from many faiths.[16]

CNN correspondent John Vause has written that he traveled to the school expecting to find "what some are calling an Islamic madrassa . . . like the ones that teach hate and violence in Pakistan and Afganistan." He observed, "I've been to those madrassas in Pakistan. . . . This school is nothing like that." He went on to report that "there are a lot of Christians, Buddhists, and also Confucian." The Associated Press also published an account that described the first school Obama attended his first year in Indonesia as "clearly a Catholic school."[17]

In regard to the charge that he was trained and converted to the Muslim faith as a boy, Obama responded to *ABC News*, "When I was six, I attended an Indonesian public school where a bunch of the kids were Muslim, because the country is 90 percent Muslim. . . . The notion that somehow, at age six or seven, I was being trained for something other than math, science and reading, is ludicrous."[18] Despite the charges of some, it would appear that most Americans have come to believe that Obama is not a Muslim and that he has accepted the Christian faith. In any case, while it did not seem to influence his religion, these years in his youth may have had a lasting influence on him in other respects.

In his book *Dreams from My Father*, Obama recalls a number of incidents during his experience in Indonesia. They include lessons in boxing from his stepfather and a fight with a classmate. Whatever his thoughts about these early years of his life, those who knew him during his stay in Jakarta have fond memories of him. One former teacher remembered him as being a "polite, friendly, and benevolent student."[19] Another commented that "he was one of my brightest students, especially in math." Registered as Barry Soetoro, Soetoro being the name of his Indonesian stepfather, he is remembered fondly by many.[20]

One teacher often tells the story of his writing a composition entitled "What I Want to Be When I Grow Up" and stating, "I will be President."[21] What can be concluded about President Obama's years as a student in Indonesia is that he was a fine student who is today a hero in the schools that he attended. With the help of his mother's early morning lessons, he was academically well prepared to succeed in an exclusive private school in Hawaii. Although his mother agonized about leaving him with her parents, both she and Barack were looking to ensure that he received the best education possible.

His mother was more than satisfied with the decision when he was accepted by the Punahou Academy. While living with his grandparents and attending

Punahou, Obama is described as "a good but not outstanding student." He would probably agree that his major interest during high school was his membership on the school basketball team. His coach remembered that he "never went anywhere without his basketball, a ball given to him by his absent father." The coach went on to say that "while Obama wasn't the best on the team, he might have worked the hardest."[22]

It was also suggested that his experience in sports helped him learn to communicate effectively. One of his fellow team members recalled, "He could beat anybody in a debate and we wouldn't even realize we got beat because we'd end up agreeing with him. . . . He would be very straight to the point and then he'd just have a way of just getting people to agree."[23]

A very reflective and sensitive adolescent, the future president has admitted that he "dabbled in drugs and alcohol." As a dark-skinned product of an interracial marriage, he learned what it was like to be a member of a racial minority, as there were few black students enrolled in the school. He has written, "I was trying to raise myself to be a black man in America, and beyond the given of my appearance, no one around me seemed to know exactly what that meant."[24]

The president has admitted that although his grades were good, he could have done better in high school. In any case, it can be concluded that he had the privilege from fifth grade until graduation to attend a prestigious school that has an excellent reputation in Hawaii. Founded in 1829, it was officially chartered in 1853 as "a non-profit, non-sectarian institution." As early as 1958, advanced placement college courses were added to the curriculum. By 1983, computers had become an integral educational tool in the school program.[25]

On their current website, the principal, Dr. Kevin Conway, defines the mission of the high school as follows:

> At Punahou, we are trying to build social conscience; we are trying to build global awareness; we are trying to teach creative thinking and critical thinking all at the same time. And we can do that here. Any parent who has a child at this school is giving their child a wonderful gift. We want students to graduate from here who are independent learners, who think well, who challenge assumptions, and who can put ideas together in new and creative ways."[26]

His high school made available to students a "service learning" program that offered "activities and opportunities within Punahou and the larger community." The Luke Center for Public Service at the school "provides guidance and resources to students interested in developing their own service projects." It is perhaps not surprising that even as a youth Barack Obama was beginning to think about public service. In addition, students are exposed to a chapel program which is meant to be "a source of spiritual, moral and ethical education." Finally, the school has the Wo International Center, which provides "global education opportunities for students, including programs in intensive language instruction, study abroad and summer programs, and lectures and seminars."[27]

Even if he was not always a totally conscientious student, being educated in an institution such as Punahou set Obama apart from many in his generation. There is no question that he experienced a fine college entrance program and that he probably could have been accepted in any college of his choice. In his first book he described how he selected the college he would attend. In making his decision, he admitted that at the time he was "indifferent toward college as toward almost everything else" in his life.[28]

In his biography of Obama, entitled *The Bridge*, David Remnick states that at Punahou, the future president's academic record was "unremarkable, but even though he was a B-student, his college prospects were promising. Like the best New England prep schools, Punahou routinely sent its top-tier students to the best colleges and universities in the country—and the second-tier students, Obama included, did almost as well."[29]

His college of choice was Occidental College in Los Angeles. On its website the college describes itself as "one of the oldest liberal arts colleges on the West Coast. Founded in 1887, it now touts the fact that its alumni include individuals who have led companies such as Pacific Telephone, American Express, International Banking, Weyerhaeuser Corp., and created their own successful businesses including Simple Green."[30]

In addition, the information available on the website takes pride in the fact that the college has been consistently named by *U.S. News & World Report* "as one of the most diverse liberal arts colleges in the country."[31] The website also notes that Occidental College is located in a "multi-cultural neighborhood . . . with upscale restaurants, coffee shops, and art galleries." The area is described as a "small town in a big city."[32] The neighborhood is described as an "urban oasis."[33]

It was in this "urban oasis" that Barack Obama began his college education. As he settled into undergraduate life he was conscious that his own background was different than most African Americans his age. He knew that his life would have most likely been very different if he had grown up in the Watts area of Los Angeles. It became increasingly clear to him that he was more like "the black students who had grown up in the suburbs, kids whose parents had paid the price of escape."[34]

Still, it has been observed that while at Occidental, Obama was "awakened" to the need to serve his fellow man. His fellow students saw him as, "if not the hardest worker, a serious person with an intellectual curiosity and maturity beyond his years." Another acquaintance noted, "I didn't see him ever being on the fringe. He seemed very centered and settled." A humanities professor noted that he was a "talented, thoughtful person who had concerns beyond himself."[35]

While not overly active in political causes at Occidental, Barack did take part in a demonstration that was seeking to force his college to divest itself of the stocks in companies that were dealing with the South African government. It was a way to pressure that government to end its racial segregation policy (apartheid). He told a fellow student after the rally, "That's the last time you'll ever hear another speech out of me."[36]

It is difficult to know from his book whether the young undergraduate was happy during his two years at Occidental College. He did write that "two years from graduation, I had no idea what I was going to do with my life, or even where I would live." He was looking for "a place where I could put down stakes and test my commitments." After learning about a program that Occidental had arranged with Columbia University, he decided to apply. His hope was that even "if there weren't any more black students at Columbia than there were at Oxy, I'd at least be in the heart of a true city with black neighborhoods in close proximity."[37]

In the book *The American Journey of Barack Obama*, it is reported that during his two years at Columbia, "he pushed away drugs and became a much more serious student" with a greatly increased "social conscience." Along with spending long hours studying in the library stacks, he lived in a black neighborhood and wandered around the city of New York so that he could learn more about how poor people lived. By the time he graduated, his primary ambition was to become a community organizer.[38]

Following his graduation, he was unable to find a position as a community organizer and instead took a job with the Business International Group, a global consulting firm. Obama described his brief interlude with the company this way: "I had my own office, my own secretary, money in the bank. . . . I would catch my reflection in the elevator doors—see myself in a suit and tie, a briefcase in my hand—and for a split second I would imagine myself as a captain of industry, barking out orders, closing the deal, before I remember who it was that I told myself I wanted to be and felt pangs of guilt for my lack of resolve."[39]

After quitting this job, he worked for three months "for a Ralph Nader offshoot up in Harlem, trying to convince the minority students at City College about the importance of recycling." Three months later he was unemployed and without income and "he had all but given up" on the dream of becoming a community organizer. His break came when Marty Kaufman, an experienced organizer, offered him a position in Chicago.[40]

Prior to any discussion of his time in Chicago, it would seem logical to continue to trace his formal educational experiences. After serving three years as a community organizer in Chicago, Obama applied and was accepted at Harvard Law School. The highlight of his time at Harvard was his election in 1990 as the president of the *Harvard Law Review*. As the first African American elected to this prestigious position, Obama was given wide media exposure.[41]

The importance of the honor is described by a former *Law Review* president who said that the job is "fairly disconnected with the breadth and rough and tumble of real politics. . . . It's an election among a closed group. It's more like electing a pope." In this position, Obama received high marks from his contemporaries for his political skills. The *New York Times* headlined an article in 2007 that suggested that it was in law school that "Obama Found Political Voice."[42]

In his book *Dreams from My Father*, Obama describes his years at Harvard as a time when he spent most of his days "in poorly lit libraries, poring through cases and statutes." He went on to write that "the study of law can be disappointing at times, a matter of applying narrow rules and arcane procedure to an uncooperative reality; a sort of glorified accounting that serves to regulate the affairs of those who have power." On a more positive note, he comments that "the law is also memory; the law also records a long-running conversation, a nation arguing with its conscience."[43]

Whatever his views of the law, with a magna cum laude degree from the Harvard Law School and his election as the president of the *Law Review*, Barack Obama was ending an outstanding career as a student. Along with his degree, he had a contract to write a book, and his prospects for a leadership role in our society were evident. Regarding his views on education, he had learned as a student the importance of hard work. In part because of the encouragement of his parents and grandparents he had experienced firsthand the potential of a high-quality education.

On the other hand, except for his years of living in New York City, he had not yet seen much of how less-privileged students were educated. The product of high-quality schools and colleges, he had also benefited from a family that placed a high importance on a formal education. Still, it is also true that his formal education did not expose him to public schools, community colleges, or public universities in the United States. The years he was about to spend in Chicago would greatly broaden the future president's educational experiences.

NOTES

1. Barack Obama, *Dreams from My Father* (New York: Three Rivers Press, 1995), 5.

2. *Dreams from My Father*, 9–10.

3. The Editors of *Life*, *The American Journey of Barack Obama* (New York: Little, Brown and Company, 2008), 24.

4. Ibid., 26.

5. Ibid.

6. *Dreams from My Father*, 70–71.

7. Amanda Ripley, "The Story of Barack Obama's Mother," *Time*, 9 April 2008, www.time.com/time/printout/0,8816,1729524,00.html (accessed 9 September 2009).

8. Janny Scott, "Obama's Mother Had a Varied International Career," *New York Times*, 13 March 2008, www.nytimes.com/2008/03/13/world/americas/13iht-obama.4.11053506.html (accessed 9 September 2009).

9. Ibid.

10. "The Story of Barack Obama's Mother."

11. "Obama's Mother Had a Varied International Career."

12. *Dreams from My Father*, 58.

13. Associated Press, "Barack Obama's Grandmother Dies," *MSNBC.com*, 3 November 2008, www.msnbc.msn.com/id/27522679/print/1/displaymode/1098/ (accessed 9 September 2009).

14. Ibid.

15. "The Obama File," www.theobamafile.com/obamaeducation.htm (accessed 4 September 2009).

16. "Reporters Prove Obama Never Attended Muslim School," *The Center for Grassroots Oversight*, 22 January 2008, www.historycommons.org/entity.jsp?entity=basuki_school_1 (accessed 9 September 2009).

17. Ibid.

18. Jake Tapper and Nitya Venkataraman, "Obama Goes on Campaign to Debunk Madrassa Education Allegation," *ABC News*, 24 January 2007, abcnews.go.com/print?id=2819634 (accessed 7 September 2009).

19. Mohit Joshi, "Obama Still Fondly Remembered at Indonesian School, *TopNews.in.*, 21 April 2008. www.topnews.in/obama-still-fondly-remembered-indonesian-school-237092 (accessed 7 September 2009).

20. Ibid.

21. Ibid.

22. Neal Karlinsky and Dan Morris, "The 'Rat-Ballers': Obama's High School Crew," *ABC News*, 26 April 2007, abcnews.go.com/print?id=3082803 (accessed 17 September 2009).

23. Ibid.

24. "Life before the Presidency," *Barack Obama Frontpage*, millercenter.org/academic/americanpresident/obama/essays/biography/2 (accessed 4 September 2009).

25. "The History of Punahou," *Punahou School*, www.punahou.edu/page.cfm?p=1788 (accessed 7 September 2009).

26. "Academics," *Punahou School*, www.punahou.edu/page.cfm?p=1802 (accessed 7 September 2009).

27. Ibid

28. *Dreams from My Father*, 96.

29. David Remnick, *The Bridge: The Life and Rise of Barack Obama* (New York: Random House, 2010), 98.

30. "A Long Tradition," *Occidental College*, www.oxy.edu/x2357.xml (accessed 7 September 2009).

31. "By the Numbers," *Occidental College*, www.oxy.edu/x2356.xml (accessed 7 September 2009).

32. Ibid.

33. "About Occidental," *Occidental College*, www.oxy.edu/x92.xml (accessed 7 September 2009).

34. *Dreams from My Father*, 99.

35. Scott Helman, "Small College Awakened Future Senator to Service," *Boston Globe*, 25 August 2008, www.boston.com/news/politics/2008/articles/2008/08/25/small_college_awakened_future_senator_to_service/ (accessed 7 September 2009).

36. *Dreams from My Father*, 108.

37. Ibid., 115.

38. *The American Journey of Barack Obama*, 52.

39. *Dreams from My Father*, 136.

40. Ibid., 140.

41. Jodi Kantor, "In Law School, Obama Found Political Voice," *New York Times*, 28 January 2007, www.nytimes.com/2007/01/28/us/politics/28obama.html (accessed 9 September 2009).

42. "In Law School, Obama Found Political Voice."

43. *Dreams from My Father*, 437.

2

The Chicago Years

When Barack Obama arrived in Chicago in 1985 to begin his new job, he found that he had a great deal to learn. Not only did he have to meet and get to know the people he would be working with, but he would have to engage them to determine the primary needs that might be met by organizing community members. Not everyone thinks positively about community organizers.[1]

The conservative *National Review* defined community organization: "It is the practice of identifying a specific aggrieved population, say unemployed steelworkers or itinerant fruit pickers, or residents of a particularly bad neighborhood, and agitating them until they become so upset about their condition that they take collective action to put pressure on local, state, or federal officials to fix the problem, often by giving the affected group money."[2]

The more liberal *Nation* magazine is much more positive about the work of community organizers, especially the role played by Barack Obama. It found that in interviews with the associates of Obama in Chicago, almost everyone agreed that he was "dedicated, hard-working, dependable, intelligent, inspiring, a good listener, confident but self-effacing." The publication also complimented him for being successful in training "strong community leaders while keeping himself in the background and as a strategist who could turn general problems into specific, winnable issues."[3]

Others observed that he was utilizing the organizing tradition of Saul Alinsky, a nationally known community organizer. Another colleague suggested that "it was a stretch for him to do Alinsky techniques. He was more comfortable in dialogue with people. But challenging power was not an issue for him. Lack of civility was."[4]

Although some have been critical of Obama's link to Saul Alinsky, it should be noted that when Obama arrived in Chicago, Alinsky had been dead for more than a decade. It also is true that other prominent leaders, such as Hillary Clinton, had been drawn to the man and his techniques. She, for instance, wrote an undergraduate thesis about Saul Alinsky. While the legacy of the man causes some to view him as a "left-wing" radical, his lasting contribution was to "create a set of rules, a clear-eyed and systematic approach that ordinary citizens can use to gain power."[5]

In doing this, Alinsky focused on some very practical projects, such as filling potholes in the streets, securing summer jobs for young people, removing asbestos from city apartments, and persuading the managers of these apartments "to repair toilets, pipes, and ceilings."[6] Another more infamous connection of Obama during his time in Chicago was his relationship with Bill Ayers. Although much of the talk about this issue was to be found on various blogs, it did reach the mass media during the 2008 presidential campaign.

An article carried in the *Washington Post* began with a quote by Larry C. Jackson of the *Huffington Post*. It stated, "William Ayers, in the age of terrorism, will be Barack Obama's Willie Horton." For those who don't remember the story of Michael Dukakis's pardon of William Horton, a convicted murderer, it was used by George H. W. Bush during the presidential campaign in 1988. The issue proved very detrimental to the Dukakis campaign. There were those who attempted to argue that Barack Obama's relationship with the former radical terrorist Bill Ayers would show that the Democratic candidate was also a radical.[7]

Ayers is now a faculty member in the education department at the University of Chicago, and he was there at the same time Obama was teaching at the university. As a former member of the Weather Underground, Ayers was involved in a number of violent acts. They included as many as a dozen bombings between 1970 and 1974. Despite the fact that he has reentered the mainstream of society as a college professor, he was quoted in the *New York Times* as late as 2001 as saying, "I don't regret setting bombs. . . . I feel we didn't do enough."[8]

When questioned about his relationship with Ayers as part of a presidential campaign debate, Obama dismissed any friendship, saying that he only knew Ayers "as a guy who lives in my neighborhood." The moderator continued to press the issue, and Obama did admit that he had served with Ayers on a charitable board. The candidate went on during the debate to denounce Ayers' support for violence.[9]

A CNN reporter attempted to learn how extensive the contacts between the two men had actually been. It was discovered that their paths crossed "repeatedly." Both were members of the board of the Annenberg Challenge Project, which funded educational projects, including those supported by Bill Ayers. The group gave hundreds of thousands of dollars to Ayers' small schools project, which promoted alternative education in special schools, such as the Peace School, which had a curriculum centered on a United Nations theme. The funding came directly from the Annenberg Foundation, which Obama chaired.[10]

The project was ended in 2003, and in its final report it was noted that it had resulted in "little impact on school improvement and student outcomes." The relationship between Obama and Ayers gained the national spotlight when Sarah Palin accused Obama of "palling around with a domestic terrorist." The Obama campaign called the charge "ludicrous."[11]

David Axlerod, a close adviser to Obama, admitted that the two men were friendly, but the word "pals" probably does not properly describe their relationship. Along with their work with the Annenberg Foundation, it is also true that Obama wrote a review for a book written by Ayers. The review, which appeared in the *Chicago Tribune* in 1997, was short but favorable. It concluded that the book is "a searing and timely account of the juvenile court system, and the courageous individuals who rescue hope from despair."[12]

There were other events where the two men appeared together, along with times when they attended various social occasions. Still, none of the investigations prove any specific influence that Ayers might have had or perhaps still has with Obama. It is true that the former revolutionary has not stopped being critical of our government and its programs. He was quoted in 2007 as saying,

This is the time not only of great stress and oppression and authoritarianism, and a kind of rising incipient American form of fascism, and what the government counts on, what the powerful count on, is that we will stay quiet. It's the idea that we can tolerate those intolerable things without screaming, without somehow coming out, joining up and coming out and saying something. It's what they count on in terms of keeping things under control.[13]

Whatever his past and present views are, there is no way to prove that his ideas have affected President Obama's education policies. Most observers would agree that in this area at least, as president, he has not been seeking to radically change our education system. Thus, it is now probably academic to be concerned about the influence of Bill Ayers on our nation's present educational policies. While the Ayers connection might not be significant, Obama did learn from his experience in Chicago.

His wife, Michelle, agrees that his time in Chicago as a community organizer, state senator, and college professor combined to create a turning point in his life. Mrs. Obama believes that "it helped him to decide 'how to impact the world'—assisting people in defining their mutual interests and working together to improve lives."[14]

Certainly, this time was important to him, as he spends over one hundred pages in his book *Dreams from My Father* talking about his experiences as a community organizer. His work here exposed him to the Chicago public school system. It must be remembered that up to this point in his life, he had not been involved in the problems of public education. In *Dreams from My Father*, he describes his first visits to a Chicago elementary school.[15]

Obama was taken to the principal's office by a security guard. His conversation with the principal began by her telling him about the young girl who had just left her office. The young lady was the mother of one of the students. The principal went on to tell him that she was "a junkie. Her boyfriend was arrested last night and can't make bail. So tell me—what can your organization do for someone like her?" During the course of their meeting, the principal shared the fact that "she'd set up a child-parent center that brought teenage parents into the classroom to learn with their children."[16]

As the conversation continued, the school administrator expressed her opinion that "most of the parents here want what's best for their child. . . . They just don't know how to provide it. So we counsel them on nutrition, health care, how to handle stress." In addition, her child-parent center encouraged them to read to their children. It also sought to help parents earn their high school equivalency diploma. Sometimes, these parents were even hired as teaching assistants.[17]

During a tour of the building, Barack commented on how cute and happy the six-year-olds seemed to be. It certainly appeared to him that they were enjoying school and their teacher. The principal then shared her view that "the change comes later, although it seems it's coming sooner all the time." When asked what the change was, she answered, "When their eyes stop laughing. Their throats can still make sound, but if you look at their eyes, you can see they've shut off something inside."[18]

Following this visit, Obama began spending several hours a week with children and their parents. Often his goal was to get parents involved in training at a local community college. As president, it would seem that his involvement with the Chicago public schools could have only opened his eyes to the needs of students and families in urban settings throughout the country.

Certainly, he saw decaying school buildings that needed windows and toilets repaired and schools with inadequate supplies. He could not help but compare the high schools in Chicago to the country club–like atmosphere that he experienced at his own high school. Even though this experience was not occurring until his mid-twenties, he still was seeing firsthand what most of his predecessors in the White House had never seen.

His decision in 1988 to leave Chicago to seek a law degree from Harvard was a difficult one. The authors of *The American Journey of Barack Obama* quoted the new law student as saying about his Chicago experience, "What I'd lost in youthful enthusiasm, I made up for in experience." This book, at least, expressed the view that "it is clear now that, as he progressed, he began to formulate certain of the social-action policies of his presidential bid. Some of his speeches across the land in 2007 and 2008 closely echoed talks he had given in Chicago way back when."[19]

In part, the decision to attend graduate school was, in his own words, the need to learn "things that would help me bring about real change. I would learn about interest rates, corporate mergers, the legislative process; about the way businesses and banks were put together; how real-estate ventures succeeded or failed. I would learn power's currency in all its intricacy and detail." His goal at this point was that he could bring this knowledge back to Chicago to help solve the many problems he had found there.[20]

His first reason to return to Chicago from Harvard was when he was accepted as a summer associate at the law firm Sidley Austin. It was there that he met his future wife, Michelle, in 1992. This meeting became a turning point in the lives of these two young ambitious attorneys. In many ways, the relationship that has evolved has made Michelle the person who most influences Obama's opinions on many subjects.[21]

Her place in his life is illustrated in a recent biography of Michelle, which quotes Obama as saying, "She's the boss. Gotta check with the boss." The same book describes their marriage as "consisting of two highly driven, highly intense, highly functional, highly intelligent people who believed in the same things, shared the same goals, wanted to accomplish the same social program, and who both were able to throw themselves into their work."[22]

As an informal presidential adviser, Michelle Obama herself has a very impressive resume. This might be especially true in the field of education. Michelle Robinson was born on January 17, 1964, to Fraser and Marion Robinson. Her father was employed as a pump worker for the City of Chicago Waterworks and was also a volunteer and precinct captain of the Democratic Party. Mrs. Robinson was a stay-at-home mother, who later worked as a secretary in the offices of Spiegel Catalog. She now is retired and living in the White House as part of the first family.[23]

Unlike her husband, Michelle is a product of a public school system. Her entire educational background is summarized below:

Bryn Mawr Elementary School (renamed Bouchet Academy), Chicago, Illinois, 1970–1977. Michelle Robinson was such an excellent student that she was able to skip the second grade. In 1975, while enrolled in the sixth grade, she was chosen for a "gifted student" program, which permitted her the chance to take advanced biology and French classes at Kennedy-King Community College.

Whitney Young Magnet High School, Chicago, Illinois, 1977–1981. Based on her academic excellence, Michelle Robinson was given the chance to attend the first "magnet" high school in Chicago, which afforded students a greater depth and breadth of study with a focus on college preparedness. As a student here, Michelle Robinson was enrolled in advanced-placement classes, was invited and joined the National Honor Society, and served as Student Council Treasurer.

Princeton University, Princeton, New Jersey, 1981–1985, bachelor's degree in Sociology, with a minor degree in African-American Studies. She worked with both the Third World Center and belonged to the Organization of Black Unity, an African-American student group. She graduated cum laude.

Harvard Law School, Juris doctor degree, Cambridge, Massachusetts, 1985–1988. While in attendance, Michelle Robinson joined the Black Law Students Association, which often brought speakers to campus, addressing legal issues and career guidance.[24]

Although she was a product of the Chicago public school system, there is little question that she experienced the most academically challenging program offered by the city schools at that time. Had she remained in her neighborhood high school, it is quite possible that her subsequent educational career might have been different. It is also true that her personal experience in a city magnet school might possibly be a factor in convincing President Obama to support the charter school movement.

Magnet schools have a specific academic focus. In the case of the Whitney Young School, it was a school meant to challenge students who had been identified as being educationally gifted. The charter school movement, which has been a favorite program of the Obama administration, is also an attempt to stimulate experimentation in schools and as a result, like magnet schools, charters allow students to attend schools other than those located in their neighborhood.

As to her collegiate experience, Michelle's biographer, Liza Mundy, suggests that she was not altogether comfortable at Princeton University. Michelle experienced an unpleasant situation when the mother of her freshman roommate heard that her daughter had been assigned an African American roommate. The mother petitioned the university to change the assignment.[25]

As a result of this and other experiences, Michelle's biographer observes that the young college student chose to withdraw from many possible social contacts. Her feelings were expressed in her senior thesis when she wrote: "I have found that at Princeton no matter how liberal and open-minded some of my White professors and classmates may try to be toward me, I sometimes feel like a visitor on campus; as if I really don't belong. Regardless of the circumstances under which I interact with Whites at Princeton, it often seems as if, to them, I will always be Black first and a student second."[26]

During her stay at Harvard, Michelle "would emerge as a hardworking young woman who was less outspoken and radicalized than some of her peers, but harbored a quiet commitment to social change." She did participate in one sit-in demonstration that was an attempt to "win greater minority representation on the faculty." Her most significant extracurricular activity was her work as an active member of the College Legal Aid Society, which was "essentially a student-run law firm. Students who worked there committed to spending at least twenty hours a week helping poor people with civil cases."[27]

Following her graduation from Harvard, Michelle Obama held several jobs. She began as an attorney in the law firm of Sidley Austin as an associate specializing in marketing and intellectual property. It was while working with this firm in 1988 that she was assigned to mentor Barack Obama, who had come to work as a summer intern. Four years later they were married.[28]

After the death of her father in 1991, Michelle reevaluated her goals in life and left her position with the law firm to enter the public sector. Her first position was as an assistant to Mayor Richard Daley. This was followed by an appointment as assistant commissioner of planning and development for the City of Chicago. After leaving her job for the City of Chicago, "in 1993, she founded 'Public Allies Chicago,' which provided young adults with leadership training for public service careers." This nonprofit organization was "named by President Bill Clinton as a model AmeriCorps program."[29]

Michelle left this position in 1996 and accepted a new role as associate dean of student services at the University of Chicago. The last position she held before her husband was elected president was as executive director of community and external affairs for the University of Chicago hospitals. Concerning her career path, Michelle Obama always felt that she and Barack had made the right decision in leaving corporate America. At a campaign event in Ohio, the future first lady told a group of young people, "Don't go into corporate America. You know, become teachers. Work for the community."[30]

Although it is impossible to fully know specifics of Michelle Obama's views on education, it can be concluded that it is an issue about which she feels deeply. As first lady, she made the decision several months after taking office to visit the Department of Education. Joining Secretary of Education Arne Duncan and speaking to a room full of department employees, she said, "Imagine what we can do with millions of dollars more investment in this area. We can expand opportunities in low-income districts for all students." She went on to talk about the possible improvements that could come about with the economic stimulus package.[31]

At the same meeting, she talked about her own educational background. Mrs. Obama noted that she was

> a product of people who are investing everyday towards the education of regular kids who'd grown up on the south side of Chicago, kids on the north side, folks in the south, in the west—young people who oftentimes come into these systems not knowing their own power and their own potential, believing that there's some magic out there, to do great things. . . . I wouldn't be here if it weren't for the public schools that nurtured me and helped me along.

She went on to support new initiatives in early childhood education, which has become another initiative that is being pursued by the Obama administration.[32]

Consistent with positions taken by Mrs. Obama, she has been a strong advocate of using stimulus money to "prevent layoffs and education cuts," as well as allowing schools to hire new teachers and making college more affordable.[33] In addition to her support for more educational spending, she and Barack have both been vocal on the role of parents in assisting in their children's education. Despite busy schedules, during their entire marriage, they have emphasized the importance of spending time with their two daughters. Barack Obama has admitted that he and Michelle have struggled with "how to balance work and family in a way that's equitable to Michelle and good for our children."[34]

In his second book *The Audacity of Hope*, he wrote, "It's hard to argue with Michelle when she insists that the burdens of the modern family fall heavily on the woman." After recounting the stresses in their marriage, he argues that the nation must become "serious about family values." He suggests that the best place to start is to make "high-quality daycare affordable for every family that needs it."[35]

Whether it be the issue of the role of parents or the necessary reforms in our schools, Michelle Obama has undoubtedly been and will continue to be a strong advocate concerning these issues. Thus, it is true that President Obama has an important education adviser in his own home who will continually remind him of the importance of families and schools. During his years in Chicago, his marriage and children were major considerations in causing education to become an important issue to the young aspiring politician. It was in Chicago that Barack Obama began his career in politics.

He first became a candidate for public office when he ran as a Democrat for the Illinois State Senate in 1996. At the time, he was only thirty-three years old. According to the *New York Times*, he was a progressive Democrat in "a time of Republican control." It was the conclusion of Janny Scott, who wrote the story for the *Times*, that Obama "turned out to be practical and shrewd, a politician capable of playing hardball to win elections, . . . a legislator with a sharp eye for opportunity, a strategist willing to compromise to accomplish things." The same article observed, "He courted collaboration with Republicans." It was also noted that he "endured hazing from a few black colleagues, played poker with lobbyists, and studiously took up golf."[36]

Peter Slevin, a staff writer for the *Washington Post* who studied Obama's legislative career, came to some similar conclusions. He writes of former legislative colleagues who described Obama as being "methodical, inclusive, and pragmatic. He cobbled together legislation with Republicans and conservative Democrats, making overtures other progressive politicians might consider distasteful." The *Post* story does not question that Obama is a "committed liberal," but that he learned that politics was "a full-contact sport" and he grew to not be overly concerned about "sharp elbows nor the occasional blind-side hit." Along with poker games and golf, Obama frequently played pickup basketball and participated in the party circuit in the state capital.[37]

U.S. News & World Report also published an article about Barack Obama's career as a state legislator. The reporter, Kenneth T. Walsh, wrote: "He is neither an unblemished hero living under a star with only the purest of motives, as many of his supporters hope, nor a weak-minded naïf who lacks the toughness to take on his harshest adversaries, as many of his detractors fear." For this writer, Obama was "a conventional politician who demonstrated some very unusual traits—extraordinary communication skills, the ability to grow as a leader, and the good sense and savvy to recognize a zeitgeist, the nation's powerful desire for change, when he sees one."[38]

The article also argues that during his time as a state legislator he showed himself as a person with "unbridled ambition." The person who first hired the young Obama as a community organizer is quoted as saying, "I don't think he would have ended up where he is if he hadn't come to Chicago. . . . It's where he got an incredible education in real politics. His idealism became tempered with realism and practicality very quickly."[39]

While serving in the state senate, Obama was not disinterested in the field of education, but was perhaps more active in issues such as health care and economic growth. In his early years, when the Republicans had the majority in the legislature, Obama did contribute as "a co-sponsor of a bill which restructured the Illinois welfare program. . . . He was also involved in various pieces of legislation which established a $100 million Earned Income Tax Credit for working families, increased childcare subsidies for low-income families and required advance notice before mass layoffs and plant closings."[40]

After the Democrats became the majority party in the legislature in 2002, Obama became the chairperson of the Health and Human Services Committee.

With the Democrats in control, he was able to write and pass more legislation than in previous years. Besides new laws in health care, he was successful in legislating "worker's rights laws that protected whistleblowers, domestic violence victims, equal pay for woman, and overtime pay."[41]

During his final years in the state senate, health care became his primary interest. Although his goal was to create for Illinois a health insurance system that would cover everyone in the state, according to one of his critics his approach could be described as "incremental radicalism." While he really wanted to completely overhaul the system and create a single-payer plan, he was forced by political reality to settle for some much less radical changes in the system.[42] Similar problems are likely when changing any major institution.

Despite the emphasis on health care, there are some clues as to his developing feelings about education. He was very involved in the establishment and administration of a group called the Illinois Early Learning Council. The vision of this organization is to develop "a high-quality early learning system that will be available to all children birth to five throughout the state by enhancing, coordinating, and expanding programs and services for young children." The services included would be "Pre-Kindergarten, childcare, Head Start, healthcare, and parental support programs."[43]

In regard to education, there is also a website that purports to quote State Senator Obama on his views concerning various legislation. There are three questions that relate to education as part of a document called "General Candidate Questionnaire." The first question is "Will you vote to increase state funding . . . to at least 50% of public education costs?" To reach this milestone, it would undoubtedly have been necessary to raise state taxes. Obama's answer to the question was that he would vote to increase state funding to at least 50 percent.[44]

A second question dealt with support for a voucher system, which would allow public funding for private and religious schools. Obama was opposed to any voucher system. It should be noted that although he does support charter schools, he continues to disagree with the idea of vouchers. The final question was whether he would support the right of public employees to strike. This would, of course, include teachers, and although public employee strikes are outlawed in the majority of the states, Obama supported this right.[45]

Finding specific information concerning State Senator Obama's legislative activities has been made somewhat more difficult because his personal files have not been made available. Reuters sought to obtain the files, but concluded that Obama had made a concerted effort not to have his records archived by the state. It is their opinion that he "does not want a complete paper trail of his time in the Illinois State Senate."[46]

When questioned about the records by Tim Russert on *Meet the Press* in 2007, Obama said: "Well, let's be clear, in the state senate every single piece of information, every document related to state government was kept by the state of Illinois and has been disclosed" and "is available right now." The state agency in charge of records has stated that it does not maintain Senator Obama's personal records or papers.[47]

If there has been criticism of Obama's record keeping as a legislator, there have also been those who have questioned his family's choice of schools for their daughters. Even though Michelle herself was a product of the Chicago public schools, the Obamas decided to send their children to the University of Chicago Laboratory School, founded by educational philosopher John Dewey in 1896. The school is famous for its progressive teaching methods. Currently, the annual tuition for an elementary student in grades 1 through 4 is $19,683.[48]

It is quite possible that since both of the Obamas were employees at the University of Chicago they were given special consideration for the tuition cost. Even though some would question politicians' commitment to public schools when they send their own children to an expensive private school, others would argue that it does not mean that a family does not care about public schools.

Whatever his record in the state legislature, Barack Obama was an extremely popular politician with his constituents. In his first election, he received 82 percent of the votes, and this increased to 89 percent in 2002. In his final election he ran unopposed.[49] While there is little question that he was a popular, hardworking legislator, it was extremely difficult to predict how he would react in his next job as a U.S. senator. In regard to education, it is likely that he would continue to support legislation attempting to improve public schools.

There is no question that he showed an early interest in early childhood education, which is an initiative he continues to support as president. There were few clues as to his views on many other education proposals that he would support later in his career. It should be remembered that his work in the Illinois legislature was just one activity during his final seven years in Chicago. Much of his time and energy went to his position as a professor at the University of Chicago. This part of his professional work also should be briefly considered as we attempt to further clarify his views on education.

Strangely enough, there were those during the presidential campaign who charged that Obama was falsely claiming to be a law professor at the University of Chicago. In response to this charge, the university released the following press release:

The Law School has received many media requests about Barack Obama, especially about his status as "Senior Lecturer." From 1992 until his election to the

U.S. Senate in 2004, Barack Obama served as a professor in the Law School. He was a Lecturer from 1992 to 1996. He was a Senior Lecturer from 1996 to 2004, during which time he taught three courses per year. Senior Lecturers are considered to be members of the Law School faculty and are regarded as professors, although not full-time or tenure-track. The title of Senior Lecturer is distinct from the title of Lecturer, which signifies adjunct status. Like Obama, each of the Law School's Senior Lecturers has high-demand careers in politics or public service, which prevent full-time teaching. Several times during his 12 years as a professor in the Law School, Obama was invited to join the faculty in a full-time tenure-track position, but he declined.[50]

Obama's teaching duties included a traditional course in due process and equal protection areas of constitutional law and a class in voting rights, election law, and campaign finance. He also taught a seminar on racism and the law. A *New York Times* story reported that "at a formal institution, Barack Obama was a loose presence, joking with students about their romantic prospects, using first names, referring to case law one moment and 'The Godfather' the next."[51]

A *Time* magazine article described him as "a rock-star professor with hoards of devoted students." The same story quoted a former student as saying, "There was no pontificating from on high about what we should think."[52] In another *New York Times* article, the author also talked to former students. One of them described Obama as "a street smart academic. . . . He wanted his students to consider the impact laws and judicial opinions had on real people."[53] In addition, the author reported that the student evaluations of his teaching were consistently high.[54]

As a professor for twelve years, there is little question that Barack Obama impacted the lives and careers of many students. It is also true that the experience affected him. The *Chicago Tribune* has noted that "the story people haven't talked about—in part because Barack didn't want to tell it; it was not to his political advantage—is that he spent a large part of his adult life" in his small office at the Law School. It certainly may be true that "between 1996 and 2004, his principal job was at the University of Chicago Law School. The part-time job was the state legislature."[55]

It has been observed that many of his closest advisers as president are people he met at the university. David Axelrod, who is a top political adviser of the president, is a graduate of the university, while Valerie Jarrett, a senior adviser, was a university trustee. Other Obama advisers from his work at the university are Cass Sunstein and Austan Goolsbee, Susan Sher, Christina Tchen, and Lisa Brown. Secretary of the Department of Education Arne Duncan also had connections with the university.[56]

The work of Barack Obama as a law professor, a state senator, and community organizer all contributed to preparing him for a much larger stage. In a book that he completed in 2006, he clearly articulated the views that he developed during this Chicago period of his life. The best seller *The Audacity of Hope* was published the same year as Obama was elected to the U.S. Senate. From this book and from his Senate campaign and career as a senator, we can begin to see the outline of the education program he would pursue as president.

NOTES

1. Byron York, "What Did Obama Do as a Community Organizer?" *National Review*, 8 September 2008, article.nationalreview.com/370073/what-did-obama-do-as-a-community-organizer/byron-york (accessed 21 September 2009).

2. Ibid.

3. David Moberg, "Obama's Community Roots," *The Nation*, 3 April 2007, www.thenation.com/doc/2007041/moberg (accessed 21 September 2009).

4. Ibid.

5. Ryan Lizza, "The Agitator," *New Republic*, vol. 236, issue 12, 19 March 2007, 22–29.

6. Kenneth T. Walsh, "On the Streets of Chicago, a Candidate Comes of Age," *U.S. News & World Report*, 26 August 2007, www.usnews.com/usnews/news/articles/070826/3obama.htm (accessed 21 September 2009).

7. "Obama's Weatherman Connection," *Washington Post*, 16 February 2008, voices/washingtonpost.com/fact-checker/2008/02/obamas_weatherman_connection.html (accessed 25 September 2009).

8. Ibid.

9. Drew Griffin and Kathleen Johnston, "Ayers and Obama Crossed Paths on Boards, Records Show," *CNNPolitics.com*, 7 October 2008, www.cnn.com/2008/politics/10/07/obama.ayers/ (accessed 25 September 2009).

10. Ibid.

11. Ibid.

12. "Barack Obama's Review of William Ayers' Book," *zomblog*, 18 October 2008, www.zombietime.com/zomblog/?p=64 (accessed 25 September 2009).

13. Patrick J. Reilly, "Bill Ayers," *Discoverthenetworks.org*, 2008, www.discoverthenetworks.org/individualprofile.asp?indid=2169 (accessed 25 September 2009).

14. "On the Streets of Chicago, a Candidate Comes of Age."

15. Barack Obama, *Dreams from My Father* (New York: Three Rivers Press, 1995), 232.

16. Ibid.

17. *Dreams from My Father*, 232–233.

18. Ibid.

19. The Editors of *Life*, *The American Journey of Barack Obama* (New York: Little, Brown and Company, 2008), 52.

20. *Dreams from My Father*, 276.

21. Liza Mundy, *Michelle* (New York: Simon & Schuster, 2008), 120–21.

22. Ibid.

23. "First Lady Biography: Michelle Obama," *National First Ladies' Library*, www.firstladies.org/biographies/firstladies.aspx?biography=45 (accessed 21 September 2009).

24. Ibid.

25. *Michelle*, 67.

26. Ibid.

27. Ibid., 79–83.

28. Linda Lowen, "Profile of Michelle Obama," *About.com*, womensissues.about .com/od/influentialwomen/p/MichelleObama.htm (Accessed 21 September 2009).

29. Ibid.

30. Liza Mundy, "When Michelle Met Barack," *Washington Post National Weekly Edition*, 13–19 October 2008, 9.

31. Yunji de Nies, "Michelle Obama Rallies the Education Troops," *ABC News*, 2 February 2009, blogs.abcnews.com/politicalpunch/2009/02/michelle-obama.html (accessed 25 September 2009).

32. Brian Montopoli, "Michelle Obama Visits Department of Education," *CBS News*, 2 February 2009, www.cbsnews.com/blogs/2009/02/02/politics/politicalhot sheet/entry4770188.shtml (accessed 21 September 2009).

33. Julie B. Mack,"Michelle Obama Says Spend Stimulus Money on Education," *Teachinglife*, 3 February 2009, teachinglife.today.com/2009/02/03/michelle-obama -says-spend-stimulus-money-on-education/ (accessed 23 September 2009).

34. Barack Obama, *The Audacity of Hope* (New York: Three Rivers Press, 2006), 336–42.

35. Ibid.

36. Janny Scott, "In Illinois, Obama Proved Pragmatic and Shrewd," *New York Times*, 30 July 2007, www.nytimes.com/2007/07/30/us/politics/30obama.html (accessed 28 September 2009).

37. Peter Slevin, "Obama Forged Political Mettle in Illinois Capitol," *Washington Post*, 9 February 2007, www.washingtonpost.com/wp-dyn/content/article/ 2007/02/08/AR2007020802262.html (accessed 23 September 2009).

38. Kenneth T. Walsh, "Obama's Years in Chicago Politics Shaped His Presidential Candidacy," *U.S. News & World Report*, 11 April 2008, www.usnews.com/ articles/news/campaign-2008/2008/04/11/obamas-years-in-chicago-politics-shaped -his-presidential-candidacy.html (accessed 15 September 2009).

39. Ibid.

40. "Highlights of Obama's Strong Record of Accomplishment in the U.S. and Illinois Senate," *Know the Facts*, factcheck.barackobama.com/factcheck/2008/01/14/ obamas_strong_record_of_accomp.php (accessed 28 September 2009).

41. Ibid.

42. Stanley Kurtz, "Barack Obama's Lost Years," *The Weekly Standard*, 11 August 2008, www.weeklystandard.com/content/public/articles/000/000/015/386abhgm.asp (accessed 15 September 2009).

43. "Illinois Early Learning Council," *State of Illinois*, www.illinois.gov/gov/elc/ (accessed 1 September 2009).

44. "Chicago Politics," *The Obama File*, www.theobamafile.com/obamaillinois .htm (accessed 15 September 2009).

45. Ibid.

46. "Illinois State Archives Letter Raises Questions about Obama's Records Claim," *Judicial Watch*, 27 March 2008, www.judicialwatch.org/illinois-state-archives -letter-raises-questions-about-obama-s-records-claim (accessed 30 September 2009).

47. Ibid.

48. "About the Laboratory Schools," *The University of Chicago Laboratory School*, ucls.uchicago.edu/about/ (accessed 1 October 2009).

49. "Ballots Cast—General Election," *Illinois State Board of Elections*, 3 November 1998, www.elections.il.gov/electioninformation/getvotetotals.aspx (accessed 28 September 2009).

50. "Media Inquiries," *University of Chicago Law School*, www.law.uchicago .edu/media (accessed 15 September 2009).

51. Jodi Kantor, "Teaching Law, Testing Ideas, Obama Stood Slightly Apart," *New York Times*, 30 July 2008, www.nytimes.com/2008/07/30/us/politics/30law.html (accessed 15 September 2009).

52. Steven Gray, "Taking Professor Obama's Class," *Time*, 10 September 2008, www.time.com/time/politics/article/o,8599,1835238,000.html (accessed 15 September 2009).

53. Alexandra Starr, "The College Issue Case Study," *New York Times*, 19 September 2008, www.nytimes.com./2008/09/21/magazine/21obama-t.html (accessed 28 September 2009).

54. Ibid.

55. Tom Hundley, "Ivory Tower of Power," *Chicago Tribune*, 22 March 2009, archives.chicagotribune.com/2009/mar/22/magazine/chi-mxa0322magazineobama pg6mar22 (accessed 30 September 2009).

56. Ibid.

3

The United States Senator

Work on a possible campaign to elect Barack Obama to the United States Senate began in the summer of 2003. The first step was for his chief political adviser, David Axelrod, to begin to build a national reputation for the potential senatorial candidate. His efforts led to several media stories about Obama, both in Illinois and in Washington, D.C. The theme of this publicity was that this young African American graduate of Harvard Law School was a potential political star in the making. The attention gained from this media campaign also helped raise necessary funds to finance additional advertising.[1]

Early in the Democratic primary campaign, the name of Barack Obama was not well known throughout the state. In the early polls, his support was as low as 10 percent. Fortunately for him, the frontrunners became involved in attacking each other. As the campaign heated up, his most prominent rivals had personal issues that severely reflected on their reputations and credibility. Still, it was not until the final weeks of the campaign that Obama emerged as the frontrunner.[2]

Even the members of Obama's campaign staff were pleasantly surprised when he won the primary in a race with three other candidates by receiving 53 percent of the votes cast.[3] It should be noted that during this long primary fight, education did not emerge as a major issue. When it was mentioned, it centered around the No Child Left Behind law. Obama's frequent quote regarding this important legislation was, "George Bush left the money behind."[4]

In the general election, education would be a more frequent topic of conversation. At the beginning of the campaign, it appeared that the Republicans were going to run a very formidable candidate. Jack Ryan was seen as "an articulate, movie-star-handsome, Dartmouth-educated millionaire who had actually left Wall Street to become an inner-city high school teacher." The fact that he was seen as a political moderate with strong support outside of Chicago caused commentators to suggest that he would be an effective opponent for Obama.[5]

However, Ryan was forced to quit the race, in large part because of "allegations that he had forced his ex-wife, television actress, Jeri Ryan, to visit sex clubs with him against her will." As a result of this bad publicity, he gave up the campaign and the Republican Party replaced him with an "ultraconservative black radio commentator," Alan Keyes.[6]

During the campaign, there were several points where education issues would become important. It was during this time that Barack Obama published his second book, *Audacity of Hope*. In the index, there are numerous pages that are cited as dealing with education. One theme dealt with early in the book is Obama's support of what is now often called "pay for performance" for teachers. He suggests that a truly effective teacher should be worth an annual salary of $100,000.[7]

It is interesting that he shows a preference for paying math and science teachers more, as well as giving special consideration to teachers willing to work in the "toughest urban schools." In discussing this issue, he admits that it would be difficult to come up with a fair system for evaluating teachers and that any plan must deal with more than students' test scores. It is his opinion that another aspect of an evaluation system would be peer review. He does think that agreeing upon a fair plan is not an "insoluble" problem.[8]

In another chapter, he writes about how changes in family life have created new challenges for schools. Mentioned is the fact that "half of all first marriages end in divorce" and that "60 percent of all divorces involve children." It was also noted that a third of all children are born out of wedlock. More than a third of our school children lack a father in their home. These family statistics are even higher in the African American community. For schools, our single-parent homes produce more dropouts and more teenage pregnancies. To deal with these problems, Obama calls for community-based programs, which include the establishment of "marriage education workshops."[9]

Still another section of the book deals with the need to raise money to help schools. He is clear that for him, the wealthy should pay a higher share of their income in taxes so that it can be "plowed back into education, so that the next generation has a fair chance."[10] There is no question in this book that the Democratic candidate for Senate from Illinois is committed to improving education in the United States. In a chapter titled "Opportunity," he writes the following:

Throughout our history, education has been at the heart of a bargain this nation makes with its citizens: if you work hard and take responsibility, you'll have a chance for a better life. And in a world where knowledge determines value in the job market, where a child in Los Angeles has to compete not just with a child in Boston but also with millions of children in Bangalore and Beijing, too many of America's schools are not holding up their end of the bargain.[11]

In the book, he goes on to argue that improving schools is not the job of the government alone. Parents must instill in their children a love for learning. On the other hand, government funding is important in education. For him, the disparity between schools in well-off suburbs and schools in urban and some rural communities is a national problem. One of the specific needs he cites is to provide excellent teachers in every classroom. He writes, "If we're serious about building a twenty-first-century school system, we're going to have to take the teaching profession seriously."[12]

For him, this means "changing the certification process to allow a chemistry major who wants to teach to avoid expensive additional coursework." He believes that "pairing up new recruits with master teachers . . . and giving proven teachers more control over what goes on in their classrooms" would make a positive difference.[13]

Along with his concern about public schools, he addresses the need to improve our colleges and universities. Included in the initiatives he proposed is the need to build upon our community college system. It is his belief that these two-year institutions can play a key role in making our nation more competitive. Obama recommends that the federal government should make it easier for students to pay for their college education.[14]

The fact that as a state senator, Barack Obama was thinking and writing about our national education problems was a definite indication that it was a priority issue as he sought to earn a place in the United States Senate. There were other signs of this interest during his campaign. Perhaps the key event during this period was his speech to the 2004 National Democratic Convention. As the keynote speaker of the convention, he received national exposure on the major television networks.

Although he was merely a senatorial candidate at the time of the speech, Barack Obama emerged from the convention as a rising star in the Democratic Party. In his address, he referred to the fact that his African father's "tough hard work and perseverance" had earned him a scholarship to study in this "magical place" of America. He went on to describe the dream that his parents had for him to attend "the best schools in the land, even though they weren't rich, because in a generous America you don't have to be rich to achieve your potential." Obama told a national television audience that his own story "is part of the larger story" and that "in no other country on earth is my story even possible."[15]

There is little doubt that by this time in his life, Obama had realized that his own educational opportunities had been a key component in the success that he had thus far achieved. During the speech to the convention, he mentioned individuals he had met during the campaign. One of these people was a young woman from East St. Louis, "who has the grades, has the drive, has the will, but doesn't have the money to go to college."[16]

Later in the speech, he included the line, "If there's a child on the south side of Chicago who can't read, that matters to me, even if it's not my child."[17] It would seem that his own experience in Chicago had created a passion for helping children from poor urban areas. This speech was not the only reference to education during the campaign. On October 16, 2005, Obama was interviewed by Neal Conan on National Public Radio. The transcript of the program quotes Obama as saying, "I think there's a consensus around the need to drastically ramp up our educational performance and an assessment that No Child Left Behind hasn't done the job and that there are a host of innovations that are being done at the local level that need to be reflected in national policy."[18]

During the same program, he talked about what a few years later would become a major aspect of his educational stimulus policy.

> The idea is to set up innovation districts in which we find best practices, particularly around teacher recruitment training and retraining, we put a lot of money into one district that is committed to innovation and where teachers and school board members and parents and students are willing to try significant innovation around these issues . . . and we keep on funding those things that work, and stop funding those things that don't work and then we take what we learn from these districts and apply them more broadly.[19]

As the campaign progressed, Obama's popularity rose and his opponent, Alan Keyes, became increasingly desperate and made a number of personal attacks on Obama. He labeled Obama's view of abortion as a "slaveholder's position," accused gays and lesbians of being "selfish hedonists," and claimed that Jesus would not vote for his opponent. The final results of the election were not a surprise, as Obama received 70 percent of the vote to Keyes' 27 percent.[20]

The new high-profile senator was eager to learn his new job. He told an aide when asked about his future plans, "I have no intention of running for president in 2008 and just want to get established in the Senate."[21] The plan that was agreed upon by Obama and his advisers for the first two years of his term had three phases. Initially, he would concentrate on Illinois to "earn the respect of the voters."[22]

During the first twelve months, he turned down most out-of-state speaking engagements and instead spent his weekends at thirty-eight town meetings in Illinois. Thirty-one of these sessions were in areas other than Chicago, where he already had strong support. The second phase of the plan would return his focus to the Chicago area. Finally, after shoring up the home state voters, he would become more active on the national stage.[23]

As the senator who began as ninety-ninth out of one hundred on the seniority list and a member of the minority party, Obama quickly realized the limitations of his power. While having some success in areas such as ethics reforms and nuclear proliferation, he "was surprised by the slow pace of the Senate." At the state level, he remembered that "we could get a hundred bills passed during the course of a session," but in the United States Senate "it was maybe twenty." Early on in his term of office, his harshest critics seemed to be his most liberal supporters.[24]

By the summer of 2005, Obama was becoming involved in overseas travel, as he joined with some other legislators to visit Russia. On his return, he became involved in the bipartisan support for aiding the recovery of New Orleans after Katrina. As part of the congressional election campaign in 2006, he traveled around the country and helped raise 4.4 million dollars for Democratic candidates. When the Democrats prevailed in the midterm election, Obama suggested to his closest aides that "maybe they should start to think about something bigger."[25]

After the Democrats took control of the Senate, Obama was able to exert additional influence on the legislative process. Although he was interested in a variety of issues, his seven committee assignments included membership on the Committee on Health, Education, Labor, and Pensions. There is some disagreement as to exactly what his voting record as a senator reflected. One agency classified Obama as a "rank-and-file Democrat." Another called him a "practical, common sense progressive who emphasized support for teachers and college affordability." A third called him a "Democratic Party loyalist." On the other hand, the *National Journal* ranked him in 2007 as "the most liberal senator."[26]

Perhaps the best indication is found in a website that averaged the ratings of seven liberal interest groups. This source placed him "among the most liberal."[27] In terms of education, Senator Obama received "an 'A' or a hundred percent rating from the largest teachers union, the National Education Association."[28]

About.com summarized Senator Obama's legislative accomplishments in 2007 and 2008:

- Obama has introduced 11 resolutions in this session. Of the 11 resolutions, four were passed/agreed to by the Senate. The sole joint resolution stayed in committee.

- Obama has introduced 59 bills in this session. Of the 59 bills, two—S.453 and S.2433—were placed on the Senate floor calendar. None have been voted on.
- Obama has introduced 59 amendments in this session. Of the 59 amendments, 22 were passed by the Senate, either by voice vote or unanimous consent.[29]

There were several significant education bills included in the list of laws that Obama sponsored. Among them were the following:

- A bill to authorize resources for a grant program for local educational agencies to create innovation districts.
- A bill to establish nutrition and physical education standards for schools.
- A bill to amend the Elementary and Secondary Education Act of 1965 to allow state educational agencies, local educational agencies, and schools to increase implementation of early intervention services, particularly schoolwide positive behavior supports.[30]

In addition, there was legislation dealing with authorizing funds for summer learning grants, especially for low-income students; a law to increase the rigor of middle school education; the development of a public website to help individuals learn about college scholarships; and a program to provide math, science, and engineering mentors for women and underrepresented minorities who were interested in careers in those fields.[31]

While Barack Obama's career in the Senate was certainly not primarily focused on the field of education, there is evidence that it was an area of concern for him. It is also true that during his final two years in the Senate, a good deal of his time was spent preparing to run for president. In November of 2006, the day after the Democrats won control of Congress, Obama and his advisers met in Chicago to discuss a plan that would allow him to win the Democratic nomination for president of the United States. Before anything moved forward, it was necessary to convince Michelle that Barack should pursue the nomination. When she agreed, plans were formulated for a national campaign.[32]

It was in Abraham Lincoln's own hometown of Springfield, Illinois, where on February 10, 2007, Barack Obama declared his candidacy. In the speech announcing his decision to run, he linked the "lack of textbooks and computers in schools . . . to the skewed priorities of politicians a thousand miles away." Also in this speech, he cautioned that while the government should "play a crucial role . . . more money and programs alone will not get us where we need to go."[33]

As he had done on numerous occasions, Obama called on parents to "accept responsibility for instilling an ethic of achievement in our children." In addition, the speech included a reference to the goal of making a college education "affordable." Finally, in the closing paragraphs he said, "I want to win the next battle—for better schools, and better jobs, and health care for all."[34] Barack Obama's presidential campaign, which officially began with this speech, would give even more clues as to his aspirations for transforming our nation's education system.

NOTES

1. David Mendell, *Obama: From Promise to Power* (New York: Harper Collins, 2007), 203.

2. Ibid., 206.

3. Christopher Andersen, *Barack and Michelle* (New York: Harper Collins, 2009), 213.

4. *Obama: From Promise to Power*, 225.

5. *Barack and Michelle*, 213.

6. "Barack Obama," *Answers.com*, 21 January 2009, www.answers.com/topic/barack-obama (accessed 28 September 2009).

7. Barack Obama, *The Audacity of Hope* (New York: Three Rivers Press, 2006), 162–63.

8. Ibid., 162–63.

9. Ibid., 332–33.

10. Ibid., 190.

11. Ibid., 159.

12. Ibid., 162.

13. Ibid.

14. Ibid., 163–65.

15. Barack Obama, "Reclaiming the Promise to the People," *EbscoHost*, 1 August 2004, web.ebscohost.com/ehost/detail?vid=3&hid=2&sid=bc2e33a9-c1d5-4aaf-b6d7-c4285943c13b%40sessionmgr11&bdata=JkF1dGhUeXBlPWlwLHVpZCZsb2dpbkBZ2U9TG9naW4uYXNwJnNpdGU9ZWhvc3QtGl2ZSZzY29wZT1z aXRl#db=aph&AN=14075106 (accessed 7 October 2009).

16. Deborah White, "Barack Obama's Inspiring 2004 Democratic Convention Speech," *About.com*, usliberals.about.com/od/extraordinaryspeeches/a/ObamaSpeech.htm (accessed 5 October 2009).

17. "Reclaiming the Promise to the People."

18. "Senator Barack Obama," *National Public Radio*, 26 October 2005, www.npr.org/templates/story/story.php?storyId=4975603 (accessed 12 October 2009).

19. Ibid.

20. "Barack Obama," *Source Watch Encyclopedia*, www.sourcewatch.org/index.php?title=Barack_Obama (accessed 12 October 2009).

21. Richard Wolffe, *Renegade: The Making of a President* (New York: Crown Publishers, 2009), 39.

22. Ibid., 39–46.

23. Ibid.

24. Ibid., 41–46.

25. Ibid.

26. "Obama: Most Liberal Senator in 2007," *National Journal*, 31 January 2008, nj.nationaljournal.com/voteratings (accessed 2 October 2009).

27. "109th Senate Rank Ordering," *voteview.com*, voteview.com/sen109.htm (accessed 2 October 2009).

28. "Barack Obama," *Source Watch Encyclopedia*, www.sourcewatch.org/index .php?title=Barack_Obama (accessed 2 October 2009).

29. "Obama's Senate Record: 110th Congress," *About.com*, 5 September 2008, uspolitics.about.com/b/2008/09/05/obamas-senate-record-110th-congress.htm (accessed 5 October 2009).

30. "Bills Which Obama Sponsored as a US Senator," *LexisNexis*, Job Number: 1841 : 180155787 (accessed 30 September 2009).

31. "Obama's Senate Record: 110th Congress."

32. *Renegade: The Making of a President*, 380.

33. *Change We Can Believe In: Barack Obama's Plan to Renew America's Promise* (New York: Three Rivers Press, 2008), 193–201.

34. Ibid.

4

The Presidential Campaign

Unlike in a number of past presidential campaigns, education did not emerge as a major issue either in the primaries or in the general campaign in 2008. Still, there were a number of indications in Barack Obama's speeches and campaign literature as to his general positions in the field of education. On the evening when it was announced that he had come in second in the New Hampshire primary, after congratulating Senator Clinton on her victory, he went on to say that the time had come when we must "stop sending our children to schools with corridors of shame and start putting them on a pathway to success. We can stop talking about how great teachers are and start rewarding them for their greatness."[1]

Three months later on March 18, 2008, in Philadelphia during a speech titled "A More Perfect Union," Obama said that in this election we need to

talk about the crumbling schools that are stealing the future of black children and white children and Asian children and Hispanic children and Native American children. This time we want to reject the cynicism that tells us that these kids can't learn; that those kids who don't look like us are somebody else's problem. The children of America are not those kids, they are our kids, and we will not let them fall behind in a twenty-first-century economy. Not this time.[2]

On Father's Day, he would return to a theme that he had spoken about a number of times in the past: the need for fathers, especially minority fathers, to take more responsibility for raising their children. He said,

We know the statistics—that children who grow up without a father are five times more likely to live in poverty and commit crime; nine times more likely to drop out of schools; and twenty times more likely to end up in prison. . . . We need fathers to realize that responsibility does not end at conception. We need them to realize that what makes you a man is not the ability to have a child—it is the courage to raise one.[3]

He spoke about the same issue in South Carolina when he promised to "spend more money on education," but warned that parents—especially African Americans—"needed to step up. . . . I could put all the money in the world into our schools, but if parents aren't willing to parent, there's only so much we can do."[4]

During the primary campaign, Obama also went beyond his criticism of the funding of No Child Left Behind. He began to talk about broadening the assessments used to evaluate teachers and schools. He suggested that we should "evaluate higher-order skills, including students' abilities to use technology, conduct research, engage in scientific investigation, solve problems, and present and defend their ideas." In regard to accountability, he argued that the accountability approach under a new law ought to be focused on improving schools, not punishing them. It should deal with the academic progress of the children.[5]

Later in the campaign, Obama commented on No Child Left Behind, suggesting that the law had "alienated teachers and principals instead of inspiring them." Even though he was critical, Obama was not ready to abandon the law. He believed that it could be fixed by first of all "providing the funding that was promised" and "not relying on a single, high-stakes standardized test that distorts how teachers teach."[6]

In another attack against No Child Left Behind, candidate Obama would charge that "creativity has been drained from classrooms, as too many teachers are forced to teach to fill-in-the-bubble tests." While he does not advocate the elimination of testing, he does suggest that it is just one of the ways "to make sure children are learning. It just can't dominate the curriculum to an extent where we are pushing aside those things that will actually allow children to improve and accurately assess the quality of teaching that is taking place in the classroom."[7]

His solution was to bring together "governors, educators, and especially teachers to develop better assessment tools that effectively measure student achievement and encourage the kinds of research, scientific investigation, and problem solving that our children will need to compete."[8] In a speech titled "The Call," Obama professed his support for establishing additional charter schools, improving teacher preparation programs, and developing ways to reward excellent teachers.[9]

In the general election campaign against John McCain, there were some differences between the two candidates concerning their views on education. In regard to No Child Left Behind, neither candidate called for scrapping the law, but both favored changes. As noted earlier, Obama focused on broadening the assessment process to include "higher-order skills such as problem solving, scientific investigation, and technological understanding." His other constant criticism was the inadequate funding of the law. McCain was most interested in "giving parents a greater choice in the school that their child attends." He supported vouchers that could be used for attendance at private and religious schools.[10]

Another area of concern for McCain was the testing requirement for special education students and non-English-speaking students. In any case, McCain had voted for the law and would "improve it" but not "discard it."[11] In addition, there was a difference between how the two candidates dealt with the area of early childhood education. For Obama, this issue was a top priority. He pointed out that there is a "return to society in the form of less crime, a decreased need for special education resources, higher graduation rates, better public health, and less public welfare for early childhood programs." Although McCain supported the current programs, including Head Start, Even Start, and Early Reading Services, he felt that the solution was to improve these programs, not necessarily to come up with new ones.[12]

This difference represented a common conceptual distinction between the two candidates. While Obama was willing to increase the federal role in education, McCain was more concerned about maintaining the powers of the states and local districts. Another major difference that emerged between the two candidates during the campaign was on the issue of school choice. Obama was a strong supporter of the expansion of charter schools, while McCain wished to increase parental choice to include private schools. This would be done using a voucher system.

An additional area of agreement was that both candidates supported the concept of paying teachers based on their performance, rather than their longevity in the school system.[13] There are other areas in which the two presidential candidates were very much in agreement. In the area of special education, they both felt that the federal government should be living up to the 40 percent of funding called for in the Individuals with Disabilities Act.[14]

Currently, the federal government is only supplying 17 percent of the cost of special education. Although both candidates recognized the importance of preparing outstanding teachers and some kind of merit or pay-for-performance system, their specific program proposals differed. They both also spoke in the campaign about the need to reduce dropouts, better involve parents, and improve educational technology. In looking at their specific positions, it would seem that the Democrats would undoubtedly be willing to support larger increases in federal funding for education.[15]

Judging by his presidential campaign, it would seem that the following list would summarize five of the most important aspects of Barack Obama's priorities in the field of education:

- Developing stronger curriculum standards and assessments. Obama questioned the uneven standards among the fifty states. As we will see, he will support a movement by forty-eight states to develop common curriculum standards.
- Investing in early childhood education.
- Recruiting and rewarding teachers. This focus is not only on pay for performance, but also on the development of modified certification procedures that would encourage individuals with strong academic backgrounds (especially in math and science) to pursue a career in teaching.
- Promoting innovation and excellence. For Obama, charter schools appear to be an excellent way to encourage educational innovation. He is especially critical of states that have capped the number of charter schools. This issue, along with support for paying teachers based on their performance (especially if it is partially based on students' test scores), did and will continue to place him at odds with teachers unions, which have traditionally supported Democratic candidates.
- Quality higher education programs, which should be available to all qualified students. To achieve this goal, Obama made it clear during the campaign that he was willing to spend additional federal money on college scholarships and other forms of student aid.[16]

Specifically in the area of higher education, Barack Obama as a candidate promoted the idea of creating a new service scholarship program to recruit top talent into the profession and to place these new teachers in struggling districts to teach math and science. He also suggested a $4,000 tax credit to cover two-thirds of college tuition at a public university. Junior colleges would be completely free. Students would repay the government by joining the Peace Corps. To make the paperwork easier, he would make it simple by merely placing an appropriate box on the income tax form. Finally, he would expand outreach programs for blacks, Latinos, and the poor and he would also double the funding for afterschool and summer programs.[17]

Even though education did not become one of the more important issues during the 2008 presidential election, it is clear that the Obama team had developed plans to improve our schools and colleges. The fact that he faced a major recession on assuming the presidency has undoubtedly affected any effort to carry out many of his ideas in the field of education. While an inaugural address is not meant to be merely a summary of the party platform, schools and education were mentioned in the speech. In mentioning problems facing our nation, he said, "our schools fail too many."[18] Later in the address, when talking about the work that needed to be done, he stated, "We will transform our schools and colleges and universities to meet the demands of a new age."[19] In preparing to meet this challenge, President Obama would need to begin by putting together a leadership team for the Department of Education.

NOTES

1. *Change We Can Believe In: Barack Obama's Plan to Renew America's Promise* (New York: Three Rivers Press, 2008), 210–11.

2. Ibid., 229.

3. Ibid., 234–35.

4. Richard Wolffe, *Renegade: The Making of a President* (New York: Crown Publishers, 2009), 163.

5. Anna Weinstein, "Obama on No Child Left Behind," *Education.com*, www.education.com/magazine/article/Obama_Child_Left_Behind (accessed 27 April 2009).

6. *Change We Can Believe In*, 247–49.

7. "Barack Obama on Education," *Education.com*, www.education.com/magazine/article/Barack_Obama (accessed 1 September 2009).

8. *Change We Can Believe In*, 249.

9. Ibid., 250.

10. "Public Education and the American Presidency," *Public Education Network*, www.publiceducation.org/fedupdates/2008/Oct09_special.htm (accessed 10 October 2008).

11. "Presidential Candidates on Education," *USA Today*, content.usatoday.com/news/politics/election2008/issues.aspx?i=8&c=11 (accessed 12 October 2009).

12. "Public Education and the American Presidency."

13. Ibid.

14. Ibid.

15. Ibid.

16. "The Five New Pillars of Education," *Ecoliteracy*, www.ecoliteracy.org/publications/barack_obama_education.html (accessed 28 September 2009).

17. Barbara Pytel, "Obama on Education," *Suite101.com*, 6 June 2008, educationalissues.suite101.com/article.cfm/obama_on_education (accessed 28 September 2009).

18. "Obama Inaugural Address 20th January 2009," *The Complete Text Transcripts of Over 100 Barack Obama Speeches*, obamaspeeches.com (accessed 7 October 2009).

19. Ibid.

II

THE RECORD THUS FAR

5

The Appointment of Arne Duncan

The period between the presidential election and the inauguration is a busy time for any newly elected president. Among the most important tasks during these weeks is the appointment of a cabinet. As with every other cabinet position, there was a great deal of speculation as to who might be selected as the secretary of education. Among those mentioned were former governors Roy Romer of Colorado and Jim Hunt of North Carolina.[1]

There was also speculation that governor Timothy Kaine of Virginia might be asked to consider taking the position. When quizzed by a reporter, he made it clear that he was not interested. Other potential candidates who were mentioned in the media included Kansas governor Kathleen Sebelius, former Georgia governor Roy Barnes, Stanford University education professor Linda Darling-Hammond, and even former secretary of state Colin Powell.[2] Because of her role as Obama's chief campaign adviser in the field of education, Linda Darling-Hammond was thought by some to have the advantage, as she had the future president's ear.

The name of Joel Klein, chancellor of the New York City schools, was also floated as a possibility for the appointment. Opponents of the nomination of Klein suggested that in New York City, he had followed the "blame-the-teacher-focus . . . and the mode of change supported by Bush and McCain."[3] While considering his choice, Barack Obama was dealing with an educational community that was divided into two camps. *U.S. News & World Report* defined these rival positions as the "reformers and traditionalists."[4]

The most prominent of the reformers were identified as Joel Klein and the young superintendent of the city of Washington, Michelle Rhee. They, along with others, supported such initiatives as these:

- Continued focus on testing and accountability
- Ending teacher tenure
- Paying teachers based on student outcomes

Linda Darling-Hammond, a professor at Stanford University, is considered to be a spokesperson for a more traditional approach. She and others in this camp were extremely critical of the No Child Left Behind law.[5] This group is supportive of additional federal funding focusing on the learning gaps for low-income children.[6] Rather than choose anyone who was identified with either of the competing points of view, the president-elect decided on someone who might be acceptable to the majority of the educational community.

In October 2009, *U.S. News & World Report* published a story that spoke about the way Arne Duncan had dealt with the differences between the reformers and the traditionalists. The author of the article, Richard Whitmire, wrote:

> Here's something you need to know about Duncan. Last summer, warring education camps squared off with opposing manifestos—school reformers who say vastly improved schools can rescue otherwise doomed poor kids versus social reformers who maintain that schools can't do it alone. Only one big city schools chief read over each manifesto and decided he could happily sign both: Arne Duncan.
>
> Being an adroit straddler (along with being an Obama basketball buddy) may explain how Duncan got the education secretary nod over the other contenders. Duncan won the endorsement of the very liberal American Federation of Teachers president, Randi Weingarten, and the very Republican current Secretary of Education, Margaret Spellings. Nice straddle, which is exactly what Obama appears to want from his education secretary.[7]

I am sure that President Obama would not agree with the notion that Duncan was a person without convictions who "straddled" the big issues. In introducing his choice for secretary of education, Obama called Duncan a "hands-on" leader instead of an ivory tower academic. He noted that "when faced with tough decisions, Arne doesn't blink."[8] The president went on in his remarks to say, "For Arne, school reform isn't just a theory in a book— it's the cause of his life. . . . And the results aren't just about test scores or statistics, but about whether our children are developing the skills they need to compete with any worker in the world for any job."[9]

Later in the speech announcing Duncan's appointment, Obama praised his work as the chief executive officer of the Chicago School District:

He's worked tirelessly to improve teacher quality, increasing the number of master teachers who've completed a rigorous national certification process from 11 to just shy of 1,200 and rewarding school leaders and teachers for gains in student achievement. He's championed good charter schools—even when it was controversial. He's shut down failing schools and replaced their entire staffs—even when it was unpopular. . . . In just seven years, he's boosted elementary test scores here in Chicago from 38 percent of students meeting the standards to 67 percent. The dropout rate has gone down every year he's been in charge. And on the ACT, the gains of Chicago students have been twice as big as those for students in the rest of the state.[10]

Although the reaction of most individuals and groups to Duncan's appointment was very positive, there have since been published stories that have been less than complimentary. An article in *USA Today* titled "Chicago Schools Report Contradicts Obama and Duncan" begins with the claim that "new research from a Chicago civic group takes direct aim at the city's 'abysmal' public high school performance."[11]

According to Greg Toppo, the author of the article, this report "puts a new spin on the academic gains made during the seven years that Arne Duncan led the Chicago schools." The conclusion reached in the findings was that the schools had "made little progress since 2003" and that these findings "stand in stark contrast to assertions President Obama made . . . when he nominated Duncan as education secretary."[12]

A *New York Times* article in October of 2009 also challenged Duncan's success in leading the Chicago School District. It concluded that "most students in schools that closed in the first five years of Mr. Duncan's tenure in Chicago saw little benefit." It went on to observe that "the disruptions of routines in schools scheduled to be closed appeared to hurt student learning in the months after the closing was announced."[13]

It should be noted that Duncan changed his strategy after 2006, when he chose to replace the staff of a failing school over the summer and allow the "same students to return in the fall." This report, according to the *Times* reporter, was "likely to provoke new debate about Mr. Duncan's efforts to encourage the use of Chicago's turnaround strategy nationwide." Secretary Duncan had hoped to close and overhaul one thousand failing schools and was able to gain a three-billion-dollar expenditure in the stimulus package to pay for this plan.[14]

The concerns mentioned in the articles above were not published until after the appointment was made. Following the president's nomination of Arne

Duncan, there was nearly universal support for the choice. Even a British publication would note that Duncan had "credibility with various factions in the education policy debate and would allow President Obama to avoid publicly choosing sides in that debate."[15]

Not only did he receive the endorsement of teacher unions, but the national PTA organization pointed out to its members that "Mr. Duncan, a strong advocate for parental involvement, worked in collaboration with the Illinois PTA and has demonstrated a willingness to listen and act on parent-friendly ideas and concerns. His record of raising student achievement bodes well for all America's children."[16]

The fact is that the nomination was accepted by unanimous consent by the United States Senate. This was helped by the support of Senator Edward Kennedy, chairperson of the Senate Health, Education, Labor and Pensions Committee, who said, "Arne has been a pragmatic and effective leader of Chicago's schools. . . . He's brought people together to address difficult challenges and expand opportunities so that every child can succeed." In addition, the chief educational leader in the House of Representatives, George Miller, was quoted as saying that Duncan was "a very good choice for school reform and our school children."[17]

The background of this man who gained the support of so many high-ranking officials is somewhat unique. He was born in Chicago in 1964; his parents both worked in the field of education. His father was a psychology professor at the University of Chicago, while his mother was the founding director of an after-school tutoring center for underprivileged minority adolescents on Chicago's South Side.[18]

Very early in his life, Duncan, who as an adult grew to the height of six feet four inches, became extremely interested in basketball. He often played in pickup games where he "was the only white kid." Like the two Obama daughters, Duncan attended the University of Chicago Laboratory School. It was then, as it is now, a highly ranked college preparatory program.[19]

Upon graduation, he was accepted at Harvard University, where he majored in sociology. By his sophomore year, he was a starting forward on the college basketball team. He was known as a good all-around player and in his junior year, he was among the team leaders in scoring, rebounds, and assists. Before returning for his final year as an undergraduate, he spent the next twelve months doing research for his senior thesis project, which was titled "The Values, Aspirations, and Opportunities of the Urban Underclass." While doing the research for this paper, Duncan worked as a tutor in his mother's after-school program.[20]

Although he would go on to administer the nation's third-largest school system, this experience as an after-school tutor was the only time he engaged in any type of teaching. Duncan returned to Harvard for his senior year with a passionate interest in helping underprivileged children. During his final year at Harvard, he was named cocaptain of the basketball team and became interested in pursuing a career in professional basketball.

Beginning in 1987, he would spend the next four years playing basketball professionally in Australia. During this period of his life, he maintained an interest in working with children. An acquaintance in Australia observed, "You could see he really had a soft spot for kids. . . . We had a school program that Arne practically ran for us. There was a glow of energy about him. If he was doing a clinic, he would do it right."[21]

After leaving Australia in 1992, Duncan returned to Chicago to become director of the Ariel Education Initiative, a program designed to enrich the educational experiences of children on the South Side of Chicago. In 1999, he was hired by the Chicago public schools as an assistant to the CEO, Paul Vallas. When Vallas left that position, Mayor Richard M. Daley appointed Duncan to the top position in the school system.[22]

During his work in Chicago, Duncan became actively involved in the community. He served on numerous boards including Chicago Cares, the Children's Center, the Golden Apple Foundation, the Illinois Council against Handgun Violence, Jobs for America's Graduates, Junior Achievement, the National Association of Basketball Coaches Foundation, Renaissance Schools Fund, Scholarship Chicago, and the South Side YMCA. He was also a member of the board of overseers of Harvard College.[23]

Despite his involvement in causes related to children, when he was appointed chief executive officer of the Chicago city schools, the *Chicago Tribune* pointed out his lack of a strong background in public education. While he had worked for three years as a mid-level administrator in the district, the newspaper noted that "he never had a high enough post to merit his own secretary."[24]

Despite what might be considered a very limited exposure to public education, it should be noted that according to Duncan's biography as published by the United States Department of Education, he was able during his period of leadership of the Chicago school system to unite "education reformers, teachers, principals, and business stake holders behind an aggressive reform agenda that included opening over 100 new schools, expanding after-school and summer learning programs, closing down underperforming schools, increasing early childhood and college access, dramatically boosting the caliber of teachers, and building public-private partnerships around a variety of education initiatives."[25]

Specifically, the Department of Education publication points to the fact that 66.7 percent of the district's elementary students were able to meet or exceed state reading standards. This was the highest percentage in the history of the tests. The math percentage was even higher, at 70.6 percent. It was also noted that high school students gained on the ACT examination at "three times the rate of national gains."[26]

This, along with increased graduation rates and scholarships, was given as a further indication of the progress made under Duncan's leadership. The faculty of the schools were urged to seek National Board Certification, and the number of teachers achieving "the highest education credential available to teachers increased from 11 in 1999 to 1,191 in 2008."[27]

Despite what appears to be an impressive record, there were some who were extremely disappointed in Duncan's leadership. A Chicago teacher, Jesse Sharkey, was quoted as saying, "In the past couple of years, Duncan has been turning public schools over to private operators—mainly in the form of charter and contract schools. . . . Duncan has also resuscitated some of the worst 'school reform' ideas of the 1990s."[28]

An education professor from the University of Illinois, Kevin Kumashiro, has noted that Duncan's policies have been "steeped in the free-market model of school reform that feeds the drop-out rate, increases segregation, and does little if anything to increase student achievement." For this critic at least, Duncan's tenure has been characterized by "less parental and community involvement in school governance, less support for teacher unions, less breadth and depth in what and how students learn as schools place more emphasis on narrow high-stakes testing."[29]

This type of criticism did not reach or affect the members of the United States Senate, where with the strong endorsement of Richard Daley, the mayor of Chicago, the two senators from Illinois, and both the president and the vice president, the Senate approved his appointment by unanimous consent. Prior to his official confirmation, Duncan gave testimony before the Committee on Health, Education, Labor, and Pensions of the United States Senate.[30]

It is perhaps in his opening statement at this hearing that one can best identify the ideas that might guide his actions as secretary of education. His views on the importance of education in our society are seen in this excerpt from his testimony:

> Education is also the civil rights issue of our generation—the only sure path out of poverty and the only way to achieve a more equal and just society. In a world where economic success is tied more closely than ever to educational opportunity, we are condemning millions of children to be less than they could be by consigning them to schools that should be so much more. That is a blight on our country. . . . Children have one chance for an education and children

who are in school now need a better education today if they are to thrive and succeed tomorrow.[31]

He went on to outline what he called the "bold agenda" that would be pursued by President Obama. The first item mentioned was early childhood education. He suggested that "too many children show up for kindergarten already behind. Many never catch up." He then listed Obama's proposal, Zero to Five, which calls for

- greater supports for working parents with young children,
- early-learning challenge grants to states,
- voluntary universal preschool quality enhancements, and
- more resources to build on the successes of Head Start and Early Head Start.[32]

The second initiative listed was a proposal to improve teacher quality. Here he spoke about programs that would encourage outstanding teachers to work in difficult schools, career advancement programs that would allow outstanding teachers to become instructional leaders, and "compensation based on performance." A third goal would be to increase dramatically the high school graduation rate, which is now only about 70 percent. In doing so, the administration would also be striving to raise the academic standards of all our schools.[33]

Another priority mentioned in Duncan's remarks dealt with making "sure that our citizens have the means and the encouragement to aim for education and training beyond high school." He pointed out that nearly half of the money spent by the federal government on education is being used to help Americans afford to attend college. Specifically, he pointed to an Obama proposal to give a tax credit of $4,000 for college "in exchange for one hundred hours of community service."[34]

Finally, he spoke briefly on the problem of the reauthorization of No Child Left Behind. His comments gave little clue as to the specific changes that the administration would seek in the law, but he did note that he had

seen first-hand the impact of the federal law on our students and schools. I have seen the law's power and its limitations. I agree with the President-elect that we should neither bury NCLB nor praise it without reservation. . . . I support the core goals of high standards for all—black and white, poor and wealthy, students with disabilities, and those who are just learning to speak English. Like President-elect Obama, I am committed to closing the achievement gaps, raising expectations, and holding everyone accountable for results.[35]

Unfortunately for the Obama administration, many of the educational initiatives supported by the secretary of education and the president would have to be at least temporarily set aside. The crisis created by the worldwide economic recession would, of necessity, become the first priority of the new administration. Obama would begin his offensive against the recession by proposing measures that would save many of our failing financial institutions. This would be followed by a gigantic stimulus package to try to revive the economy. The fact that a significant portion of the money, which was meant to jump start the economy, would be spent on schools and colleges clearly demonstrates the commitment of the president to the field of education. An examination of the guidelines established for spending the stimulus money allotted to education will also offer clues as to the priorities of the president.

NOTES

1. Michele McNeil and Alyson Klein, "Your Education Road Map to State and Federal Politics," *Politics K–12*, 8 August 2008, blogs.edweek/campaign -k-12/2008/08/ed_sec_watch_arne_duncan.html (accessed 23 October 2009).

2. "VA Governor Turns Down Possible Obama Appointment," *USA Today*, 4 December 2008, www.usatoday.com/news/politics/2008-12-04-kaine_N.htm (accessed 23 October 2009).

3. Duane Campbell, "Oppose the Appointment of Joel Klein as Secretary of Education," *Petition Online*, www.petitiononline.com/camp/campd227/petition.html (accessed 23 October 2009).

4. Eddy Ramirez, "Leader of Chicago Schools Is Obama's Choice for Education Secretary," *U.S. News & World Report*, 16 December 2008, www.usnews.com/blogs/ on-education/2008/12/16/ (accessed 23 October 2009).

5. Ibid.

6. Glenn Cook, "Duncan Looks Right for the Job," *American School Board Journal*, February 2009, 6.

7. Richard Whitmire, "Obama Education Secretary Arne Duncan Must Deal with Rhee, Union," *U.S. News & World Report*, 23 October 2009, www.usnews.com/ articles/opinion/2008/12/19/obama-education-secretary-arne-duncan-must-deal -with-rhee-union.html?pagenr=2 (accessed 23 October 2009).

8. Bill Meyer, "Obama Names Arne Duncan Education Secretary," *National News*, 16 December 2008, www.cleveland.com/. . ./obama_names_arne_duncan _educat.html (accessed 23 October 2009).

9. Debbi Wilgoren, "Chicago Schools Chief to Be Education Secretary," *Washington Post*, 16 December 2008, voices.washingtonpost.com/44/2008/12/16/Chicago _schools_chief_to_be_ed.html (accessed 23 October 2009).

10. Ibid.

11. Greg Toppo, "Chicago Schools Report Contradicts Obama and Duncan," *USA Today*, 12 July 2009, www.usatoday.com/news/education/2009-07-12 -chicagoschools13_N.htm (accessed 20 July 2009).

12. Ibid.

13. Sam Dillon, "Report Questions Duncan's Policy of Closing Failing Schools," *New York Times*, 28 October 2009, www.nytimes.com/2009/10/29/education/29schools.html?_r=1&hpw (accessed 29 October 2009).

14. Ibid.

15. Daniel Nasaw and Suzanne Goldenberg, "President-Elect Obama Names Arne Duncan as Education Secretary," *guardian.co.uk*, 16 December 2008, www.guardian .co.uk/world/2008/dec/16/barack-obama-arne-duncan-education-secretary (accessed 23 October 2009).

16. Jan Harp Domene, "National PTA President Reacts to Appointment of Education Secretary," *PTA*, 17 December 2008, www.pta.org/2485.htm (accessed 23 October 2009).

17. "Obama Taps Arne Duncan for Education Post," *CBS News*, 16 December 2008, www.cbsnews.com/stories/2008/12/16/politics/main4671087.shtml (accessed 23 October 2009).

18. "Arne Duncan," *Current Biography*, 2009, Biography Reference Bank Selection, Web, 2 November 2009 (accessed 26 October 2009).

19. Ibid.

20. Ibid.

21. Bob Ryan, "Hoop Journeyman Duncan, a Go-to-Guy on Obama's Team," *Boston.com*, 21 December 2008, www.boston.com/sports/colleges/mens_basketball/articles/2008/12/21/hoop_journeyman_duncan_a_go_to_guy_on_obamas_team/ (accessed 23 October 2009).

22. "Arne Duncan," Wikipedia, en.wikipedia.org/wiki/Arne_Duncan (accessed 23 October 2009).

23. Lynn Sweeton, "Arne Duncan to Be Named Obama Education Secretary," *Chicago Sun-Times*, 15 December 2008, blogs.suntimes.com/sweet/2008/12/arne _duncan_to_be_named_obama.html (accessed 23 October 2009).

24. Amy D'Orio, "The Outsider Comes In," *District Administration*, August 2002, www.DistrictAdministration.com (accessed October 2009).

25. "Arne Duncan, U.S. Secretary of Education—Biography," ED.gov, www.ed .gov/news/staff/bios/duncan.html (accessed 23 October 2009).

26. Ibid.

27. Ibid.

28. "Obama Picks School-Privatizing Union-Buster for Education Secretary," *rabble.ca*, 26 December 2008, www.rabble.ca/babble/international-news-and -politics/obama-picks-school-privatizing-union-buster-educatino-secreta (accessed 23 October 2009).

29. Ibid.

30. "Testimony of Education Secretary-Designate Arne Duncan before the Committee on Health, Education, Labor, and Pensions, United States Senate," *Senate*

.gov, 13 January 2009, help.senate.gov/Hearings/2009_01_13/Duncan.pdf (accessed 4 November 2009).

31. Ibid.
32. Ibid.
33. Ibid.
34. Ibid.
35. Ibid.

6

The Economic Stimulus Package
and Race to the Top

Months before Barack Obama took office, it was being suggested that the American economy was facing "the worst conditions . . . since the Great Depression."[1] When he did begin his administration in January of 2009, there was no question that both the world economy and that of the United States were in a state of decline. Despite the early measures taken by the administration, the recession continued into 2009. By October of 2009, the Bureau of Labor Statistics reported that since "December 2007, the number of unemployed persons has increased by 7.6 million to 15.1 million, and the unemployment rate has doubled to 9.8 percent." Millions more were under-employed or had given up looking for work.[2]

In an article published in *Economy Watch*, it was noted that during January of 2009, the Commerce Department had reported that in the final quarter of 2008, our economy had depreciated at a rate of 3.8 percent. One of the major reasons for this was that exports from the United States had decreased at the rate of 23.6 percent.[3] This decline was a clear indication that the recession was not occurring just in the United States, but throughout the world. Along with growing unemployment and declining exports, the recession was having a major impact in banking, housing, overall production, and the stock market. *Business Week* reported in February of 2009 that the economic "sentiment" in the United States was "deeply depressed."[4]

There was little question as Barack Obama assumed office that the most urgent problem facing his administration was the economy. While the president, Congress, and the Federal Reserve would first move to rescue the financial institutions and the housing industry, they were at the same time planning to infuse billions of dollars into the economy to stimulate needed growth and to save jobs. The so-called stimulus package was designed as a two-year project to revive the faltering economy. One of the primary questions facing our government was how this money should be spent. The president's commitment to educational reform would be clearly demonstrated as he recommended to Congress that a significant percentage of the stimulus money be spent on schools.

The section of the law titled "State Stabilization Funds" allotted nearly $40 billion to schools and colleges. This money was meant to help offset cuts that states, local school districts, and colleges were making in their budgets. There were also special grants available for educational technology, education of homeless children, and $250 million to improve statewide data systems. Another special grant program of $200 million was created to help states carry out Obama's plan to "set up alternative teacher compensation systems."[5]

While the federal government was making additional aid available, governors and state legislatures were still grappling with the effects of the recession on their revenue sources. The decline in income and sales tax revenues was forcing states to make significant budget cuts. Since the single largest expenditure in most states is for education, one would expect that this area of the budget would not escape careful scrutiny. At the same time, in order to receive federal funds, states were expected to not use federal aid to replace their own sources of revenue.

This dilemma was highlighted in an article appearing in the *Councilgram*, a newsletter of the New York State Council of School Superintendents. Titled "Race to the Cliff?" the article carried the subtitle "Schools Face Competing Demands—Cut Costs, Raise Performance." The author, Robert Lowry, referred to the fact that in October of 2009, New York State was faced with a deficit of more than $3 billion in the current budget. Governor David Paterson was asking the legislature to approve a further reduction in state aid to education of $686 million.[6]

Still, without the stimulus money to save jobs, the situation would have been much worse. *Teacher Magazine* reported in its October 2009 issue, "Teachers appear to have benefited most from the effort to save jobs."[7] A White House press release in October 2009 claimed that a total of 650,000 jobs in the U.S. economy had been saved by the stimulus package. Of that number it was reported that 325,000 were in the field of education. These were primarily teachers' jobs that would have been cut by their school districts without the infusion of federal funds.[8] The state that seems to have benefited the most in this effort to maintain teaching positions was California, where 62,000 teachers were able to keep their jobs.[9]

Reactions to the announcement claiming the large number of jobs saved in education were mixed. Republicans pointed to the fact that the national unemployment rate continued to rise, even with the billions spent to create or save jobs. Democrats countered by arguing that schools would have been dramatically affected without the influx of federal money. To bolster its case, the Obama administration was able to call upon the Republican governor of California, Arnold Schwarzenegger, to offer an endorsement on the positive impact of the program in his state. He was quoted in the *New York Times* as saying, "Some of our colleagues are saying it hasn't done much, or was a waste of money. . . . Well, I would dispute that."[10]

In answer to the charge that the teachers' jobs that had been saved were not real, the governor replied, "No, those teachers would have been gone, if it wouldn't have been for the federal stimulus money."[11] Despite endorsements such as this, there were a number of challenges in the media to the statistics concerning the number of jobs that the federal government claimed were saved.

A story published in the state of Washington claimed that 24,000 of the 34,500 saved positions reported for that state "probably weren't in danger in the first place." The *News Tribune* suggested that these teachers would have kept their jobs as a result of aid from Washington State's general fund. It was argued that rather than cut school aid, the state legislature would have reduced other budget categories. Federal government officials responded by pointing out that the figures they had published had come directly from the state government in Washington.[12]

Overall, despite the differences over the number of jobs saved, most observers would agree with an *Education Week* article that stated, "It's clear that the stimulus package averted tens of thousands of teacher layoffs nationwide, and mitigated deep cuts to school programs."[13] An even more all-encompassing concern with the school funding portion of the stimulus package was the need for states to maintain their own contribution to schools.

In September of 2009, the office of the inspector general of the United States Department of Education in an "Alert Memorandum" titled "Potential Consequences of the Maintenance of Effort Requirements under the American Recovery and Reinvestment Act State Fiscal Stabilization Fund" stated, "In accordance with the requirements in the ARRA, States must submit an application that includes a number of assurances in order to receive the first portion of their SFSF allocation. One assurance is that the State will maintain its support for elementary and secondary education, as well as other public institutions of higher education (IHEs), at least at the level of support for fiscal year (FY) 2006."[14]

The inspector general's action made it clear that "President Barack Obama did not intend for state lawmakers to simply cut state education spending and replace it with stimulus money." Secretary Duncan actually charged that "some states are flouting the President's wishes." He said on a number of occasions that the administration's education stimulus funding was "intended to supplement local education dollars, not replace them." In addition, he has warned that "when the spending reports are made public . . . states will be held accountable by the public and the department on how they used education funding."[15]

These threats were made real when the Inspector General named Connecticut, Massachusetts, and Pennsylvania as state governments that were "undermining the school improvement aims of the American Recovery and Reinvestment Act in their use of fiscal-stabilization funds to avert or minimize cuts in their education budget."[16]

Along with their concerns about the conditions forced upon them to receive federal aid, the states have complained about the length of time it has taken to receive the money. Secretary Duncan defended his department by pointing out that they had been sending out responses in "four to six days' time. We aren't operating like a traditional federal bureaucracy. . . . We're moving rapidly here and we're going to challenge districts and states to be equally responsive." Because of the complexity of the paperwork required, it has taken state governments a considerable amount of time to complete their applications.[17]

The other problem inherent in the procedure is that once the states receive funding, they must work with local districts to ensure that they have followed the appropriate guidelines for receiving the aid. On the other hand, much of the money was remaining with the state governments to fill the gaps caused by cuts in their own bureaucracy. *Education Week* reported that 87 percent of the federal aid was being used by the state governments.[18]

Even with the extra money from Washington, the budget reductions in some states were dramatic. The *Los Angeles Times* reported that "the impact of California's budget cuts has varied from school to school," but in the city of Los Angeles it has caused severe problems. In some city schools, "classes are crammed with about fifty students, leaving some pupils to sit on desks or the floor and their teachers to grade hundreds of papers."[19]

Despite such conditions, in some of our major cities, the problem could get worse when these new federal funds cease to be available. Currently, the infusion of federal dollars is scheduled to last only for two years. In an article in *Education Week,* it is noted that "amid a still-shaky economy, a troubling reality is starting to set in for states and school districts. The budget situation may get a lot worse when the federal economic-stimulus spigot runs dry."[20]

The hope is that within the next year the recovery will occur and states' and local school districts' tax receipts will increase. There are a number of economists who are not optimistic that the economy will recover that quickly.

If they are right, state income and sales tax revenues may not grow and the same result is likely for local property taxes. Even with the current infusion of federal aid, *Education Week* reported in October 2009 that school districts in California, Florida, and New Mexico are requiring teachers to take unpaid days off.[21]

Perhaps the most dramatic reductions have occurred in President Obama's home state of Hawaii. Initially, it was the intention of the legislature to close the public schools for seventeen Fridays during the second semester. This would have reduced the school year to 163 days of instruction, rather than the normal 180-day calendar followed in most states. The teacher unions in the state voted to approve this measure in order to avoid massive layoffs. This occurred even though 66 percent of the schools in the state have failed to meet their "Adequate Yearly Progress" goals as mandated by the No Child Left Behind law.[22]

Although schools in many areas are going through difficult times, the new federal funds have been welcomed by the states. Even so, there has been constant questioning of the most publicized aid to education program, which the administration labeled the "Race to the Top."

In August of 2009, the *New York Times* published an article titled "Dangling Money, Obama Pushes Education Shift." Sam Dillon, the journalist who wrote the article, began the story by writing, "Holding out billions of dollars as a potential windfall, the Obama administration is persuading state after state to rewrite education laws to open the door to more charter schools and extend the use of student test scores for judging teachers."[23]

These conditions were set if states were to become eligible to compete in a program called "Race to the Top." A total of $4.3 billion was set aside for this program. Because there were conditions placed on receiving the money, it created conflict between the teachers unions and the administration. Despite their strong support of Obama during the election, the unions were especially critical of the requirements forcing states to repeal any laws that prohibited the use of student test scores in evaluating teachers.

A National Education Association official expressed the union's concern when he wrote, "We cannot support yet another layer of federal mandates that have little or no research base of success and that usurp state and local government's responsibilities for public education." In addition, states with limits on the number of charter schools to be allowed were being required to lift such a cap in order to be eligible for the Race to the Top funds. For the unions, both of these restrictions seemed to be associated with programs that had been pursued by the Bush administration.[24]

Even though there was teacher opposition to these conditions, the unions did agree with the four "assurances" or objectives of the stimulus legislation.

These included the need "to improve teacher and principal effectiveness, turn around the lowest-performing schools, bolster standards and assessments, and update data systems." Despite the agreement on these goals, *Education Week* predicted that "strife" between the administration and the unions was "all but inevitable." It was even suggested that there might be legal challenges to the restrictions on receiving aid.[25]

The same publication in a different article highlighted other problems inherent in this competitive grant program. It was pointed out that states could expect to spend 642 hours filling out the required application. This concern was understandable when one considers the thirty-five-page draft of guidelines that was provided to the states. The challenge was even greater because many states had to lay off some of the professional staff who might have been expected to write the grant applications. To help with this issue, "the Seattle-based Bill & Melinda Gates Foundation hand-picked states to receive up to $250,000 each to hire consultants to help them fill out their applications."[26]

In response to the complexity of the applications, *Teacher Magazine* published an article titled "What Teachers Need to Know about Race to the Top." The article outlined the criteria for receiving state grants, but also focused on how these factors affected the issue of teacher quality. The author concluded that teachers in states receiving aid "could see significant changes in their practice, ranging from curriculum reforms to new ways of using student data to plan instruction."[27]

For *Teacher Magazine*, the most important changes will occur because of the "emphasis on revamping teacher-quality systems including recruiting, retention and compensation." More than ever, these factors will be affected by student achievement data. In describing the goals for Race to the Top, the program's director wrote that "in particular, we want schools and districts to know which teachers are effective (as measured in significant measure by how their students are improving academically), and to ensure that local decision makers use this information to inform their key decisions."[28]

As early as April of 2009, Secretary Duncan was giving out clues as to ways schools could profitably use Race to the Top funds. Included were suggestions for each of the three major aid-to-education programs. They included the following:

Title I

- Identify and use effective teachers as coaches and mentors.
- Create summer programs for algebra and other college-prep courses.
- Partner with colleges and nonprofit groups to create early-college programs.

- Close low-performing schools and reopen them with new staffs, new programs, and additional learning time.

State Fiscal Stabilization Fund

- Create new, fair, reliable teacher-evaluation systems based on objective measures of student progress and multiple classroom observations.
- Train educators to use data to improve instruction.
- Purchase instructional software, digital whiteboards, and other interactive technologies and train teachers in how to use them.

Individuals with Disabilities Education Act

- Offer training and dual certification for teachers of English-language learners and students in special education.
- Implement online individualized education programs (IEPs) aligned with state academic standards.
- Hire transition coaches to help graduating high school seniors find employment or get postsecondary training.[29]

Both the president and the secretary of education have made it clear that the federal funds being made available through the Race to the Top program are not to "support the status quo." They are looking to improve student achievement and narrow achievement gaps. In addition, their goals include creating more effective teachers and principals, ensuring that new data is used to inform decisions, and reforming the "lowest performing schools."[30]

While the Race to the Top funding only represents a small percentage of the total money being allotted for education, it has caused the most discussion in the media.[31] As states moved to meet the criteria concerning pay for performance and charter schools, the program became a major issue in many states. The effort did receive favorable comments, such as an editorial in the *New York Times* suggesting that Education Secretary Arne Duncan had "revitalized the school-reform effort that had lost most of its momentum by the closing days of the Bush administration."[32]

The same editorial cautioned the secretary that "he will need to resist those pressures and choose substantive, innovative proposals that stand the best chance of improving the schools. For that, he will need courage, stamina, and cover from the White House."[33] On November 10, 2009, the *New York Times* published another article in which it quoted Frederick Hess, the education director of the conservative American Enterprise Institute, as saying, "States are rushing to stitch together grant proposals that will win points, but many could just turn out to be short-term political plays."[34]

As they were seeking additional funds, states were also being asked to identify "current efforts and new plans for upgrading standards and assessments, building student performance data systems, improving teacher quality, and turning around low-performing schools."[35] Even with these challenges, most states entered into a fierce competition for Race to the Top funds. *Education Week* has highlighted the fact that no president in our history has had this amount of money available at his discretion for schools.[36]

Only Secretary Duncan and the president, not Congress, will decide which states receive grants. By developing the conditions for receiving the money, the administration has been able to move forward in reaching its objectives of allowing the establishment of more charter schools and pay-for-performance plans for teachers.[37]

In order to quiet the opposition of teachers unions, the final guidelines for the program were modified. The result was that Dennis Van Roekel, president of the National Education Association, was quoted as saying that the final rules "put more emphasis on student growth, teacher practice, and improving instruction. So I'm really pleased that they listened."[38] After announcing fifteen finalists at the end of March 2010, the federal Department of Education made public the two winners of the first round of competition for Race to the Top funding. Delaware will receive $100 million and Tennessee, $500 million. This decision came as a great surprise, as only a small portion of the more than $4 billion available was given out in this first round.[39]

The *Washington Post* suggested that one of the most important factors affecting the choice was the input of teachers unions into the applications.[40] Representatives from a number of states felt that this was unfair, as it was much more difficult in larger states to gain the support of "100 percent of school districts and local teachers unions."[41]

Others praised the decision. An editorial in the *New York Times* stated, "Washington has historically talked tough about requiring states to reform their school systems in exchange for federal aid, and then caved in to the status quo when it came time to enforce the deal. The Obama administration broke with that tradition this week." The fact that many of the states did not totally adhere to the qualifications for the aid resulted in a very limited use of the allotted funds during the first round. It is hoped that the fact that there is over $300 million available for the second round will cause states to work hard to fully meet the requirements announced by the Education Department.[42]

The work done by the Obama administration in providing aid for education was also praised in both the *New York Times* and *Washington Post*. In a column in the *Times*, David Brooks wrote in regard to the Race to the Top that "the news is good. In fact, it's very good. Over the past few days, I've spoken to people ranging from Bill Gates to Jeb Bush and various education reformers. They are all impressed by how gritty and effective the Obama administration has been in holding the line and inciting real education reform."[43]

Brooks also notes that even Republican Newt Gingrich has praised President Obama on his emphasis on pay for performance and charter schools. Obama has also enlisted the backing of liberal civil rights leader Al Sharpton. Conservative columnist Brooks ends his editorial with additional positive words for the president, saying that he "understood from the start that this would only work if the awards remain fiercely competitive. He has not wavered. We're not close to reaching the educational Promised Land, but we may be at the start of what Rahm Emanuel calls The Quiet Revolution."[44]

Similar praise was present in a column by Ruth Marcus in the *Washington Post*. She was especially enthusiastic about the plan to offer $97 million in 2009, and as much as $446 million in 2010, to provide "higher pay to teachers and principals who improve performance in high-poverty schools." For her at least, "on education, the administration gets high marks for its first semester. The final exam is still to be administered."[45]

Certainly not everyone agrees with the education policies of the Obama administration during its first year in office. On the other hand, few would doubt that the president is serious about his goal to improve our schools. This was shown clearly by the amount of stimulus money that was allotted to education. It is much too early to predict the results of these initiatives, but not too soon to suggest the nature of the educational policies that are likely to be put forward by the administration in the future. In examining the plans for reform in education, perhaps the best place to begin is with the consistent strong support that has been given to the charter school movement.

NOTES

1. Bill Bonner, "The Worst Conditions for the U.S. Economy since the Great Depression," *Daily Reckoning*, 14 March 2008, www.dailyreckoning.com.au/worst -conditions-for-the-us-economy-since-the-great-depression/2008/03/14/ (accessed 3 November 2009).

2. "Employment Situation Survey," *Bureau of Labor Statistics*, 2 October 2009, www.bls.gov/news.release/empsit.nr0.htm (accessed 3 November 2009).

3. "U.S. Economic Conditions," *Economy Watch*, www.economywatch.com/ economic-conditions/us.html (accessed 3 November 2009).

4. Rick MacDonald, "Jobs: Another Jumbo Decline in January," *Business Week*, 4 February 2009, www.businessweek.com/print/investor/content/feb2009/pi2009024 _771594.htm (accessed 3 November 2009).

5. Kevin Butler, "Shot in the Arm," *District Administration*, April 2009, 21–22.

6. Robert Lowry, "Race to the Cliff?" *Councilgram*, October 2009, 1.

7. "Teachers Benefit Most from Stimulus," *Teacher Magazine*, 13 October 2009, www.teachermagazine.org/tm/articles/2009/10/13/teachersbenefitstimulus_ap.html ?tkn=qmmdsssgw1n8iwfithkw7ao%2fu6ayqmouyf8h (accessed 16 October 2009).

8. Michael Cooper, "White House Chalks Up 650,000 Jobs to Stimulus," *New York Times*, 30 October 2009, www.nytimes.com/2009/10/31/us/31stimulus.html?hp (accessed 30 October 2009).

9. Ibid.

10. Michael Cooper and Ron Nixon, "Schools Are Where Stimulus Saved Jobs, New Data Show," *New York Times*, 30 October 2009, www.nytimes.com/2009/10/31stimulus.html?_r=1&ref=education (accessed 2 November 2009).

11. Ibid.

12. Melissa Santos, "Fewer Local Jobs Saved by Federal Stimulus Than Reported," *News Tribune*, 31 October 2009, www.thenewstribune.com/news/local/story/936585.html (accessed 2 November 2009).

13. Michele McNeil, "Dueling Objectives Mark Stimulus at Halfway Point," *Education Week*, 5 February 2010, www.edweek.org/ew/articles/2010/02/10/21mtr_stim -overview.h29.html (accessed 8 February 2010).

14. "Potential Consequences of the Maintenance of Effort Requirements under the American Recovery and Reinvestment Act State Fiscal Stabilization Fund," *U.S. Department of Education Office of the Inspector General*, September 2009, www .ed.gov (accessed 12 November 2009).

15. "IG Questions Use of Stimulus Aid for Education," *Education Week*, 2 October 2009, edweek.org/ew/articles/2009/10/01/304315usstimulusschools_ap.html?tkn=m . . . (accessed 2 October 2009).

16. Catherine Gewertz, "States Stung by Criticism on Use of Federal Aid," *Education Week*, 19 October 2009, www.edweek.org/ew/articles/2009/10/12/08backfill .h29.html (accessed 21 October 2009).

17. Michele McNeil, "Stimulus Aid's Pace Still Slow," *Education Week*, 17 June 2009, 26.

18. Ibid.

19. Mitchell Landsberg, "Budget Cuts Push Some Classrooms Way over Capacity," *Los Angeles Times*, 20 September 2009, www.latimes.com/news/local/la-me-ed -cuts20-2009sep20,0,2312077.story (accessed 25 September 2009).

20. Erik W. Robelen, "'Funding Cliff' Looms Large for States," *Education Week*, 30 October 2009, www.edweek.org/ew/articles/2009/10/30/10cliff_ep.h29.html (accessed 30 October 2009).

21. "In Hawaii, School's Out for Recession," *Education Week*, 19 October 2009, www.edweek.org/ew/articles/2009/10/19/307900bchischoolsfurloughs_ap.html (accessed 20 October 2009).

22. Ibid.

23. Sam Dillon, "Dangling Money, Obama Pushes Education Shift," *New York Times*, 16 August 2009, www.nytimes.com/2009/08/17/education/17educ.html?_r=3&emc =t&tntemail0=y (accessed 19 August 2009).

24. Stephen Sawchuck, "NEA at Odds with Obama Team on Stimulus," *Education Week*, 25 August 2009, www.edweek.org/ew/articles/2009/08/25/02nea.h29.html (accessed 28 August 2009).

25. Ibid.

26. Michele McNeil, "Hurdles Ahead in 'Race to Top,'" *Education Week*, 25 August 2009, www.edweek.org/ew/articles/2009/08/13/01stimcapacity.h29.html (accessed 31 August 2009).

27. "What Teachers Need to Know about Race to the Top," *Teacher Magazine*, 2 September 2009, www.teachermagazine.org/tm/articles/2009/09/02/rtt_explained.html (accessed 10 September 2009).

28. Ibid.

29. Michele McNeil, "Duncan Spells Out Preferred Uses of Stimulus Aid," *Education Week*, 15 April 2009, www.edweek.org/ew/articles/2009/04/07/29stim-spend.h28.html?tkn=u[nfmhgxyoilhfmssllbpkive%2blqloz5jgqn (accessed 15 April 2009).

30. Joanne Weiss, "Education's 'Race to the Top' Begins," *Education Week*, 24 July 2009, www.edweek.org/ew/articles/2009/07/23/37weiss.h28.html (accessed 3 August 2009).

31. Michele McNeil, "Rich Prize, Restrictive Guidelines," *Education Week*, 10 August 2009, www.edweek.org/articles/2009/08/07/37stimrace.h28.html (accessed 31 August 2009).

32. "Mr. Duncan and That $4.3 Billion," *New York Times*, 27 September 2009, www.nytimes.com/2009/09/28/opinion/28mon2.html?_r=1&ref=opinion (accessed 2 October 2009).

33. Ibid.

34. Sam Dillon, "States Compete for Federal School Dollars," *New York Times*, 10 November 2009, www.nytimes.com/2009/11/11/education/11educ.html?_r=1&hp (accessed 10 November 2009).

35. "Race to the Cliff?" 2.

36. "Race to the Top Forcing School Change," *Teacher Magazine*, 4 November 2009, www.edweek.org/tm/articles/2009/11/04/rttschoolchange_ap.html?tkn=qsxfrxhzk... (accessed 5 November 2009).

37. Ibid.

38. Sam Dillon, "After Criticism, the Administration Is Praised for Final Rules on Education Grants," *New York Times*, 12 November 2009, www.nytimes.com/2009/11/12/education/12educ.html (accessed 12 November 2009).

39. Michele McNeil, "Delaware and Tennessee Win Race to Top," *Education Week*, blogs.edweek.org/edweek/campaign-k-12/2010/03/st_st_and_st_win_race_to_the_t.html (accessed 16 April 2010).

40. Nick Anderson, "Input of Teacher Unions Key to Successful Entries in Race to the Top," *Washington Post*, 3 April 2010, www.washingtonpost.com/wp-dyn/content/article/2010/04/02/ar2010040201022.html (accessed 6 April 2010).

41. Sam Dillon, "States Skeptical about 'Race to Top' School Aid Contest," *New York Times*, 4 April 2010, www.nytimes.com/2010/04/05/education/05top.html?ref=education (accessed 6 April 2010).

42. "Enforcing School Standards, at Last," *New York Times*, 30 March 2010, www.nytimes.com/2010/03/31/opinion/31wed1.html (accessed 6 April 2010).

43. David Brooks, "The Quiet Revolution," *New York Times*, 22 October 2009, www.nytimes.com/2009/10/23/opinion/23brooks.html?_r=1 (accessed 30 October 2009).

44. Ibid.

45. Ruth Marcus, "Obama's Quiet Success on Schools," *Washington Post*, 22 September 2009, www.washingtonpost.com/wp-dyn/content/article/2009/09/22/ar2009092203009_2 . . . (accessed 25 September 2009).

7

Charter Schools

As already noted, one of the major conditions created by the Obama administration for eligibility to receive Race to the Top funds was the requirement that states lift any caps restricting the number of charter schools in the state. Largely as a result of pressure from teachers unions, a number of state legislatures had placed a limit on the number of charter applications that could be approved in their state. Due to the mandate that these caps had to be eliminated, it is expected that the number of charter schools will continue to increase.

The question as to why the president chose to force this concession on states can only be explained by the fact that it is the conviction of both the president and the secretary of education that charter schools are a positive way to bring about educational reform. In taking a strong position on this issue, it was undoubtedly evident to the president that he would face opposition from his party's traditional supporters, the National Education Association and the American Federation of Teachers. Both of these groups have been less than enthusiastic about the spread of charter schools. Although they have recently made an effort to organize the teachers in charter schools, the vast majority of teachers in these schools are not represented by a union.

The likely explanation for being willing to upset one's political allies is that the administration believes charter schools will be good for American education. There is little question that the president has concluded that, especially in our cities, we need to dramatically change what we are doing. The fact that these schools are freed from most of the bureaucratic restrictions placed on other public schools is undoubtedly appealing to the president. He also seems to be drawn by the fact that the introduction of charters into a large school district will create competition.

As seen in his approach to Race to the Top funds, President Obama believes that competition in education can only be helpful. This position is validated by a recent study reported in the *Wall Street Journal.* It noted that in a "study of twenty-nine countries . . . the level of competition among schools was directly tied to higher test scores in reading and math."[1] The fact that Education Secretary Duncan has been an active supporter of charter schools has most likely only bolstered Obama's support of the idea.

While charter schools do represent change, supporting their growth was still a more moderate position than that supported by his opponent in the presidential election. John McCain, along with many Republicans, was willing to create even more competition by supporting a voucher system for American education. Voucher plans most often would allow parents to make a choice between not only public schools, but also private schools, including those sponsored by a religious group.[2]

There was no doubt that this position would create a united opposition from all groups representing public schools. But even with many critics, there appears to be some evidence that voucher programs still have some support. In Florida, there are a significant number of Democrats and Republicans currently supporting "new legislation that would increase the value of the state's tax-credit vouchers." Similar plans have been introduced in Illinois and New Jersey.[3]

President Obama has never supported a voucher program, and thus it can be argued that he has taken a more middle-of-the-road position in regard to school choice. To understand the administration's support of charter schools, it is helpful to consider the mechanics and rationale for this type of school choice. One popular education textbook describes charter schools as follows:

> Charter schools are nonsectarian public schools of choice that are allowed to operate with freedom from many of the regulations that apply to traditional public schools. Groups such as parents, teachers, businesses, and community leaders can submit a proposal or a charter to the authorizing agency for permission to start a charter school. The agencies that approve charter schools vary from state to state and might include local school boards, intermediate school district boards, and state boards of education. If approved, the group submitting the charter usually is authorized to operate for some period of time, usually from 3 to 5 years. At the conclusion of that period of time, the charter can be removed if the approving agency determines that the provisions of the charter are not being met.[4]

Supporters of charter schools argue, "The freedom to operate without excessive regulation allows them to stimulate innovation and change and to be more sensitive to local needs." This includes, in many states, the right to hire teachers who may lack teacher certification. Most charter school teachers are not covered by tenure laws, and most often, their salary is based on their performance as opposed to a salary schedule. It is also argued that these schools can be more cost effective because the large districtwide bureaucracy is not needed.[5] In addition, this lack of interference by central office administrators can reduce the amount of paperwork required of teachers.

Opponents, on the other hand, point to the fact that charter schools draw scarce funds away from other public schools in the district. They also suggest that there are many examples of traditional public schools that are successfully functioning under district guidelines.[6]

In the ongoing debate over charter schools, another author points to the advantage of "site-based management," because it gives the individual school the ability to create a specialized educational focus. Proponents of charter schools believe that by allowing a school to make its own decisions, rather than having them made at a higher bureaucratic level, policies can be made that are most appropriate for the individual school. Those who worry about this type of independence suggest that charter schools too often have insufficient oversight.[7]

Another textbook includes a summary of the pros and cons of charter schools. Their list is as follows:

Pros	Cons
1. Provides parents and students with a choice in the public school system.	1. Can ignore the national education goals and state goals and content standards in developing their programs.
2. Permits each school to determine its philosophy and curricular emphasis with a coherent academic mission and high standards.	2. May be controlled by for-profit firms that impose standardized programs with limited school choice.
3. Increases the heterogeneity of students in schools attracting private school students into the charter schools.	3. Fail to provide teachers with the same salaries and fringe benefits they would receive in the public schools.
4. Have an image of being smaller and safer than the typical public school.	4. Have encountered fiscal accountability and management problems in the use of public funds.
5. Gives teachers greater freedom and the challenge of starting and designing a program for a new school.	5. Do not have the perceived independence because they are still a part of the public education system and thus are subject to changes in local and state requirements.[8]
6. Have been given operational and programmatic freedom in return for results-based accountability.	

While the original idea for charter schools has been traced back to Ray Budde in the 1970s, it was not until the beginning of the 1990s that charter schools became widely discussed. Ironically, a high-profile proponent at that time was the president of the American Federation of Teachers, Albert Shanker. It was Shanker's hope that charter schools would be a way for teachers to start their own schools free of administrative interference.[9]

The first charter school was begun in the state of Minnesota in 1991, and one year later another one was established in the state of California. By 2002, the federal government had begun encouraging the movement. As part of the No Child Left Behind law, $300 million was made available to "aid local and state governments to support charter schools." They were also listed as an "optional choice for parents with children in low-performing schools."[10]

As states allowed the formation of charter schools, applications were sought by a variety of individuals and groups. Although Albert Shanker had expected that charter schools would most likely be established by teachers, it has been various community groups who have been unhappy with their public schools that have most often sought charters. The vast majority of these applications have come from urban areas, where the public schools are too often perceived as failing many of their students.[11]

More recently, a number of private for-profit companies have been seeking to begin schools. Initially, it was organizations such as the Edison Project that were first to enter the competition. By 1998, the Edison Project operated forty-seven schools. Other early entries into the market were Advantage Schools Inc. and Education Alternatives Inc.[12] More recently, "the best-known and highest-profile charter management organizations" are Knowledge Is Power Program: Always Mentally Prepared (KIPP AMP) and the Accelerated School Charters in Los Angeles.[13]

The fact that companies are earning profits from public funds is especially disturbing to supporters of the traditional public school system. The companies themselves argue that they can bring management skills to their charter schools which are lacking in the bloated administrative networks of many school districts.[14]

The American Federation of Teachers has been especially concerned about the growing number of for-profit charter schools, arguing:

• They enroll few students with disabilities and spend little money on special education.
• They spend more on administration and less on instruction.
• They do not innovate but use a standardized school design, curriculum, and technology package provided by the company.

- Teachers are disgruntled about the lack of professional opportunities for advancement.
- Teachers complain about not being involved in school decision making.[15]

The National Education Association, which is the largest teacher organization in the United States, agrees with the American Federation of Teachers and has included in its policy statement that "private for-profit entities should not be eligible to receive a charter."[16]

Despite the lack of enthusiasm of the teachers unions, it is now estimated that there are more than 4,900 charter schools in forty states and the District of Columbia. These schools enroll more than 1.5 million students.[17] Currently, the city of Detroit has thirty thousand children attending forty-nine charter schools. In addition, in the suburbs of the city there are twenty thousand students who are also attending charter schools. In Detroit, charter school attendance now includes about one-third of the school-age population.[18]

Los Angeles has also been extremely active in encouraging the formation of charter schools. A new initiative in that city is aimed at opening as many as 250 such schools. Not everyone in Los Angeles is enthusiastic about this initiative. An editorial in the *Los Angeles Times* titled "Charter Schools Hold Promise, But They're No Magic Bullet" concluded with this warning: "Charter schools have played an important role in reform, and the best of them have transformed the educational futures of their students. But so far, they have not proved a panacea for what ails public education."[19]

New York City currently has even more charter schools than Los Angeles and Detroit. Its charter schools have recently been the subject of a major study that has given encouragement to the supporters of such schools. In September of 2009, *Education Week* published an article entitled, "N.Y.C. Charters Found to Close Gaps." The eight-year study, conducted by researchers from Stanford University, demonstrated that "New York City's charter schools are making strides in closing achievement gaps between disadvantaged inner city students and their better-off suburban counterparts."[20]

Unfortunately for the proponents of charter schools, the findings of another major research study published at almost the same time as the New York research were more negative. This study, also done by a group from Stanford University, known as the Center for Research on Educational Outcomes (CREDO), included schools from fifteen states and the District of Columbia. Unlike the study in New York, this research found a "wide variation in student achievement among charter schools and determined that, more often than not, students in traditional public schools were outperforming their charter school peers."[21]

Adding to the difficulty of comparing student learning outcomes, the CREDO study found that preschool children "entering charters scored nearly eight percent higher" on the entrance exam than the district average. The authors suggested that "families who are motivated enough to seek out and apply to charter schools may also tend to be more engaged in their children's education." It was also noted in the final report that it is extremely difficult to measure such things as a family's educational motivation. On the other hand, the head start of some students noted in the CREDO study did not hold up in another research project conducted in Ohio. This one also found "charter school students performing at or below the levels of students enrolled in district schools."[22]

How students are chosen for attendance in charter schools continues to be a disputed issue. One critic has written that "my beef with charter schools is that most skim the most motivated students out of the poorest communities and many have disproportionately small numbers of children who need special education or who are English-Language Learners."[23]

Supporters of charter schools respond by pointing out that in most states, if the number of students seeking to enroll in a charter school exceeds the number of places available, a lottery system must be employed. In the very favorable New York City study mentioned earlier, 94 percent of the students were admitted to the city charter schools as the result of a lottery. The report itself states that "this is a true 'apples-to-apples' comparison. Lottery-based studies are scientific and reliable. There are no other methods of studying the achievement of charter school students that have reliability that is in the same ballpark."[24]

Despite such claims, critics continue to find fault with the charter school movement. The *Washington Post*, in an article headlined "Charter School Growth Accompanied by Racial Imbalance," refers to a civil rights project that concluded that the charter school movement was creating even more racial segregation than what was already occurring in public schools.[25] Another criticism is discussed in an article published by *Education Week* that claims charter schools have a smaller percentage of students with disabilities. The article states, "These schools may appear to produce superior results, but they do so without serving comparable populations."[26]

There also has been good news for those who advocate charter schools. In a different kind of study that was not based on test scores, there was evidence that "students who attended public charter schools were 7 to 15 percentage points more likely than regular high school students to graduate and 8 to 10 percentage points more likely to attend a two- or four-year college."[27]

While future debates about charter schools are inevitable, it is helpful to consider the findings of the Center on Reinventing Public Education. This group refers to the conclusion of Julian Betts and Y. Emily Tang: "There is strong evidence that charter schools are outperforming other public schools in many ways." At the same time, their analysis indicates

- Charter school studies are highly varied in quality. The maxim caveat emptor ("let the buyer beware") applies here: Only about a third of all charter school studies can be trusted to give a fair picture of whether students are better off in a charter school or not.
- High-quality studies are more likely than weaker studies to find positive school results on student learning, in both reading and math.
- Even high-quality studies show tremendous variability in results. Charter schools perform much better in some localities than others. Elementary charter schools, in general, appear to outperform charter middle and high schools.[28]

This source concludes: "In the long run, the success of the charter movement will depend on whether it is able to build on successes and abandon failures. To reinforce success and eliminate failure, we need to understand what explains these variations. A second generation of achievement research in these areas is urgently needed."[29]

Another research group has come to a similar conclusion. The *Public School Review* has concluded:

Charter schools have shown promising, but mixed results over the years. Though more data is needed to get the overall picture, more or less the schools are faring well. On one hand there are success stories where some charter schools receive renewals of their charters because they have met the goals of their charter. On the other hand, there are schools whose charters have been revoked due to lack of proper financial management or lack of achievement.[30]

Although the results of the research have been inconsistent, the Obama administration will undoubtedly continue to support the spread of charter schools. At the same time, it is most likely that teachers unions, as well as other public school employees, will remain skeptical. This could change if the current campaign to unionize charter school teachers is successful.

Until and unless this happens, there will be headlines such as "Too Many Charter Schools Here." This was the view of a union leader in Buffalo. He remains skeptical about additional charter schools even though five of the charter schools in Erie County have joined a state teachers union. For Richard

Iannuzzi, the president of the New York State United Teachers, "Buffalo has, unfortunately, more than reached a saturation point. . . . It makes it almost a side-by-side school district, and you can't function like that." Of the 130 charter schools in New York State, 21 have become unionized.[31]

Whatever the results of the organization efforts of the unions in charter schools, it remains clear that President Obama is committed to the expansion of the charter school movement. Additional research will occur in an effort to clarify the impact of this initiative, but during the immediate future, the number of charter schools will increase. It can also be expected that more private for-profit companies will be seeking charters. It is possible that this could accelerate another program favored by the Obama administration. An editorial in the *Washington Post* raised the possibility that charter schools might provide an excellent model on teacher pay.[32]

Because most charter schools do not have unions with which to negotiate salary schedules, the management of these schools has the freedom to devise systems that attempt to tie teacher salaries to performance. Some of these models might help other public schools develop their own systems. This is undoubtedly a major goal of both President Obama and Secretary Duncan. Creating pay-for-performance plans that will be acceptable to teachers unions is a topic that will be explored in the next chapter.

NOTES

1. Paul E. Peterson, "Charter Schools and Student Performance," *Wall Street Journal*, 16 March 2010, online.wsj.com/article/sb10001424052748703909804575123470465841424.html (accessed 16 March 2010).

2. Lesli A. Maxwell, "Expansions of State Voucher Programs Gain Momentum," *Education Week*, 25 February 2010, www.edweek.org/ew/articles/2010/02/25/23voucher_ep.h29.html.

3. Ibid.

4. David G. Armstrong, Kenneth T. Henson, and Tom V. Savage, *Teaching Today: An Introduction to Education*, 8th ed. (Upper Saddle River, N.J.: Pearson, 2009), 68.

5. Ibid.

6. Ibid.

7. Sara Davis Powell, *An Introduction to Education: Choosing Your Teacher Path* (Upper Saddle River, N.J.: Pearson, 2009), 43.

8. L. Dean Webb, Arlene Metha, and K. Forbis Jordan, *Foundations of American Education*, 5th ed. (Upper Saddle River, N.J.: Pearson, 2007), 341.

9. Joel Spring, *American Education*, 12th ed. (Boston: McGraw Hill, 2006), 167.

10. Ibid.

11. "Corporate-Sponsored Public Schools," *CorpWatch*, 8 July 1998, www.corp watch.org/article.php?id=3028 (accessed 19 November 2009).

12. Ibid.

13. Stephen Sawchuk, "Unions Set Sights on High-Profile Charter-Network Schools," *Education Week*, vol. 28, no. 33 (10 June 2009), 1.

14. *American Education*, 167–68.

15. *American Education*, 173.

16. "The U.S. Education System: Special Needs and Charter Schools," *InfoUSA*, infousa.state.gov/education/overview/charter_schools_history.html (accessed 19 November 2009).

17. Gary Miron and Leigh Dingerson, "The Charter School Express: Is Proliferation Interfering with Quality?" *Education Week*, 2 October 2009, *www.edweek.org/ ew/articles/2009/10/07/06miron.h29.html* (accessed 6 October 2009).

18. Rochelle Riley, "It's Time to End the Charter School Fight," *Detroit Free Press*, 11 September 2009, www.freep.com/article/20090911/COL10/909110389/ It%5C-s-time-to-end-the-charter-school-fight (accessed 18 September 2009).

19. "Charter Schools Hold Promise, but They're No Magic Bullet," *Los Angeles Times*, 30 November 2009, www.latimes.com/news/opinion/la-ed-charters30 -2009nov30,0,1269410.story (accessed 1 December 2009).

20. Debra Viadero, "N.Y.C. Charters Found to Close Gaps," *Education Week*, 22 September 2009, *www.edweek.org/ew/articles/2009/09/22/05charter.h29.html* (accessed 23 September 2009).

21. Debbie Viadero, "More on Charter Schools: Debates and New Findings," *Education Week*, October 2009, blogs.edweek.org/edweek/inside-school-research/ charter-schools/ (accessed 15 October 2009).

22. Ibid.

23. Diane Ravitch, "Obama and Duncan Are Wrong about Charters," *Education Week*, 16 November 2009, blogs.edweek.org/edweek/Bridging-Differences/2009/11/ obama-and-duncan-are-wrong-abo.html (accessed 19 November 2009).

24. Caroline M. Hoxby, Sonali Muraka, and Jenny Kang, "How New York City's Charter Schools Affect Achievement," *The New York City Charter Schools Evaluation Project*, September 2009, vii.

25. Nick Anderson, "Study: Charter School Growth Accompanied by Racial Imbalance," *Washington Post*, 4 February 2010, www.washingtonpost.com/wp-dyn/ content/article/2010/02/03/ar2010020303959.html (accessed 12 February 2010).

26. Thomas Hehir, "Charters: Students with Disabilities Need Not Apply?" *Education Week*, 26 January 2010, www.edweek.org/ew/articles/2010/01/27/19hehir _ep.h29.html (accessed 1 February 2010).

27. Debra Viadero, "Study Gives Charters an Edge," *Education Week*, 10 February 2010, blogs.edweek.org/edweek/inside-school-research/2010/02/most_studies _of_charter_school.html (accessed 12 February 2010).

28. Julian Betts and Y. Emily Tang, "National Charter School Achievement Is Promising Overall, but Highly Varied," *Center on Reinventing Public Education*,

December 2008, www.crpe.org/cs/crpe/view/csr_pubs/254 (accessed 19 November 2009).

29. Ibid.

30. Grace Chen, "What Is a Charter School?" *Public School Review*, 4 December 2007, www.publicschoolreview.com/articles/3 (accessed 19 November 2009).

31. Peter Simon, "Too Many Charter Schools Here, Union Leader Says," *Buffalo News*, 8 October 2009, www.buffalonews.com/cityregion/story/821270.html (accessed 19 October 2009).

32. Jay Mathews, "Charter Schools Provide Good Model on Teacher Pay," *Washington Post*, 1 June 2009, www.washingtonpost.com/wp-dyn/content/article/2009/05/31/ar2009053102236.html (accessed 15 June 2009).

8

Pay for Performance or Merit Pay for Teachers

Pay for performance or merit pay for teachers and school administrators has been adopted by the Obama administration as one facet of its attempt to improve our schools. Support for this initiative is based on the conviction that we must improve teaching and that this can be done in part by rewarding excellence. It is believed that financial incentives for teachers will not only increase academic achievement in our schools, but also induce more of our nation's best and brightest people to enter the teaching profession. Both the president and Secretary of Education Duncan have argued that the way we currently compensate most teachers is inappropriate.

In the vast majority of school districts today, teachers are paid based on negotiated salary schedules under which they are rewarded with automatic increments based on years of service in the district. Along with the regular salary schedule, they might also receive added compensation for advanced degrees or additional graduate work. Contracts almost always pay teachers extra for advising extracurricular activities or coaching interscholastic sports.

The result of such a system is that older, experienced teachers receive more than double the salaries of new teachers. Critics of this system frequently point out that often the less experienced teachers are more effective than those who earn a much higher salary for doing the same job. Those who oppose the present system suggest that because raises are automatic, there is little motivation for teachers to improve what they are doing.

In addressing this issue, it is important to note that there have been a variety of approaches introduced for paying teachers based on factors other than experience. Education.com has identified the following four methods:

- Pay for performance. These are bonuses based on assessments of student learning.
- Hard-to-staff-school pay. This money is given to teachers working in at-risk schools.
- Skill-shortage pay. This money is given for teaching subjects that are difficult to staff, such as math, science, technology, and special needs.
- Advanced-role pay. This is compensation for teachers taking on leadership roles as mentors for other teachers at their school.[1]

In July of 2007, as a United States Senator, Barack Obama "endorsed the idea of merit pay for teachers before an audience hostile to the idea, the giant National Education Association." In doing so, he made clear that he wished to "work with teachers" to accomplish this goal. He assured the nine thousand delegates present, "I want to work with teachers, I'm not going to do it to you, I'm going to do it with you."[2]

Still, as with the issue of charter schools, Obama faces great skepticism from both major teachers unions concerning the concept of merit pay. The fact that he is serious about this issue was made clear in the requirements mandated to states for eligibility to receive Race to the Top funds. In a number of states, teachers had been concerned that they would be evaluated primarily on the basis of student test scores.[3]

To ensure that such a system was not adopted, states had created laws or policies against using student test scores to evaluate teachers. In order to receive federal funds under Race to the Top, the states are forced to repeal such laws or policies. Secretary Duncan defended the administration's position, saying, "Test scores alone should never drive evaluation, compensation, or tenure decisions. That would never make sense. . . . But to remove student achievement entirely from evaluation is illogical and indefensible."[4]

While Duncan was speaking to a National Education Association Convention in 2009, the delegates enthusiastically endorsed his support of increased federal funding for schools, better training for administrators, and increased mentoring experiences for teachers. On the other hand, he was "booed and hissed" when he suggested the need to consider test scores as a way of determining teacher pay.[5]

The NEA does support teacher bonuses for advanced degrees, additional certification from the National Board for Professional Teaching Standards, extra pay for teacher mentors, and bonuses for teachers willing to accept assignments in hard-to-staff schools. It does not endorse "higher salaries for math and science teachers or for performance-based pay." Most of all, it is opposed to the "use of test scores in pay or evaluation decisions."[6] Given the opposition of the National Education Association, as well as the American

Federation of Teachers, a consensus agreement on the concept of pay for performance for teachers will be difficult. Even with this reluctance, it would appear that currently, many people both in and out of government would support the arguments given for the introduction of some form of merit pay in our schools. Several of the prominent arguments were summarized by columnist Beth Lewis. They include the following:

- Americans value hard work and results, and our capitalist system hinges upon rewarding such results. Most professions offer bonuses and salary increases to exemplary employees. Why should teaching be the exception? The fact that a sloppy teacher and a dedicated teacher earn the same salary just doesn't sit right with most people.
- Incentivized teachers will work harder and produce better results. What motivation do teachers currently have to go above and beyond the job's basic requirements? The simple possibility of extra cash would most likely translate into smarter teaching and better results for our children.
- Merit Pay programs will help recruit and retain the nation's brightest minds. It's the odd teacher who hasn't considered leaving the classroom and entering the corporate workplace for the twin benefits of less hassle and more money potential. Particularly intelligent and effective teachers might reconsider leaving the profession if they felt that their extraordinary efforts were being recognized in their paychecks.
- Teachers are already underpaid. Merit Pay would help address this injustice. Teaching is due for a renaissance of respect in this country. How better to reflect the esteemed way we feel about educators than through paying them more? And the highest performing teachers should be first in line for this financial recognition.
- We are in the middle of a teaching shortage. Merit pay would inspire potential teachers to give the profession more consideration as a viable career choice, rather than a personal sacrifice for the higher good. By tying teaching salaries to performance, the profession would look more modern and credible, thus attracting young college graduates to the classroom.
- With American schools in crisis, shouldn't we be open to trying almost anything new in the hopes of making a change? If the old ways of running schools and motivating teachers aren't working, perhaps it's time to think outside of the box and try Merit Pay. In a time of crisis, no valid ideas should be quickly denied as a possible solution.[7]

The opposition to such plans from teachers is often predicated on their belief that the current ways that teachers are evaluated are ineffective and often unfair. To add the element of student test scores, they feel would only make the system worse. Traditionally, the primary responsibility for judging a teacher's work has been left to school administrators. Often, a principal is expected to supervise dozens of teachers in diverse classroom settings. Even with the help of assistant principals, and in larger districts, department chairpersons, a typical nontenure teacher might have no more than three class observations a year.

For a tenure teacher, it might only be a single observation. The administrator might be observing a Spanish class, where no English is spoken, even though the observer is unfamiliar with Spanish. The administrator could be a former English teacher observing a calculus class, where he or she has little understanding of the subject matter being taught.

Other districts have experimented with peer evaluation, where members of a secondary school department or of an elementary faculty judge each other's work. The concern here is that such an approach can create unhealthy competition and stress within a group of teachers who should be working together as a team. At the high school level, some schools have considered the use of student input. Critics of such an approach fear that this would lead teachers to seek popularity rather than academic excellence and that it could also contribute to grade inflation.

Of all of the suggestions being made by the Obama administration, perhaps the one that most disturbs teachers is that student test scores should be considered as a factor in determining a teacher's salary. Many faculty members point to the fact that test scores are greatly affected by the type of students that are assigned to the classes. A teacher who has a class with a significant number of gifted students has a great advantage over one who has been assigned a preponderance of slower children.

Students experiencing health or family problems at the time when tests are given also could bring down the examination results. There is also concern that teachers would be more likely to focus on merely "teaching to the test." Because many teachers feel that what they do in the classroom cannot be easily evaluated in the same way as other jobs in our society, there remains great reluctance in the profession to support pay-for-performance plans.

A compromise plan called the "career ladder" has been introduced in some districts. Such a plan is an attempt to create a system similar to that which is used in colleges and universities. Teachers in these institutions can advance through a series of job titles, which allows them to increase both their prestige within the institution and also their salaries. In most colleges, a teacher can advance through a group of job titles such as instructor, assistant professor, associate professor, and professor. Each promotion places the teacher in a higher salary category. A similar system, using different titles, has been attempted in some school districts. It could include titles such as instructor, master teacher, and teacher mentor.

The problem with such a system remains how to develop an evaluation system that can be used to determine promotions. Along with teaching effectiveness, college professors are most often also judged on their scholarly output. Using scholarship as a criterion for public school teachers is not likely to be considered appropriate. It is also true that in higher education, teaching is often judged in part by student evaluations. This is not a tool that could be easily utilized at most levels in our public schools. Still, the career ladder concept has been one that teachers unions have been willing to consider.

Whether it is a career ladder or some other form of pay for performance, the primary concern for most teachers is linking salary to student test results. In an article published in *Education Week*, Justin Snider considered the idea of somehow using numbers to determine the effectiveness of a teacher. He ends his article this way:

> Every educator knows that teaching is less like open-heart surgery than like conducting an orchestra, as the Stanford University professor Linda Darling-Hammond has suggested. "In the same way that conducting looks like hand-waving to the uninitiated," she says, "teaching looks simple from the perspective of students who see a person talking and listening, handing out papers, and giving assignments. Invisible in both of these performances are the many kinds of knowledge, unseen plans, and backstage moves—the skunkworks, if you will—that allow a teacher to purposefully move a group of students from one set of understandings and skills to quite another over the space of many months."
>
> Until we get much better at capturing the nuances of such a performance, we should be wary of attempts to tie teacher tenure and compensation to student test scores.[8]

A more scientific argument against the idea of pay for performance was included in the February 27, 2010, issue of *Education Week*. Debra Viadero referred to a report in *Science Daily* suggesting that "people who are driven by rewards are just as competitive, judging by their brain activity, when there's no prize in sight." The article went on to say that "contrary to the researchers' hypothesis, the brain scans showed that reward-driven subjects' brains were just as excited—in fact, even more so—when no prizes were offered." Such a study would seem to suggest that at least competitive teachers did not need merit pay to cause them to do their best.[9]

There are many others who would say that most teachers already want to do the best job possible and that a financial bonus would not have a great impact on their work ethic. In any case, the idea of merit pay for teachers is not a new one. As early as the 1920s, "40–50 percent of the districts in the United

States had some form of a merit pay plan." During the next decade, many of these were abandoned and teachers were more likely to be paid based on their experience in the district. In the 1950s, there was a resurgence of merit payment plans, and by 1968, approximately 11 percent of the nation's school districts had such systems. In the 1970s the number once again declined, to 4 percent.[10]

According to a survey by the U.S. Department of Education in 2004, "19.6 percent of districts said they rewarded some schools for excellence in teaching through a school-wide bonus or additional resources for a school-wide activity, and 15.4 percent of districts said they provide a cash bonus or additional resources to individual teachers to encourage effective teaching."[11]

Perhaps one of the reasons changes are taking place in this area is that there appears to be an increasing willingness among some teachers to entertain a pay-for-performance system. In 2007, this trend was noted by Sam Dillon in an article in the *New York Times*. He pointed out that "for years, the unionized teaching profession opposed few ideas more vehemently than merit pay, but those objections appear to be eroding as school systems in dozens of states experiment with plans that compensate teachers partly based on classroom performance."[12]

Specifically, he refers to an $86 million "teacher professionalization and merit pay initiative" in Minnesota, as well as similar smaller experiments that are under way nationwide.[13] An *Education Week* article also suggested that the new interest among teachers in merit pay was primarily among newer members of the profession. The article referred to a report released by Public Agenda and Learning Point Associates. It noted that of teachers who were thirty-two or younger, 71 percent said "they would 'strongly' or 'somewhat' favor merit pay for teachers who 'consistently work harder, putting in more time and effort than other teachers.'"[14]

On the other hand, among older teachers, only 63 percent favored "that kind of pay differentiation." It was also true that the younger teachers were more open to basing merit pay on the evaluations of principals. The same article again registered strongly the fact that a majority of teachers of all ages were skeptical about using student test scores to award merit pay.[15]

Just as the Obama initiative favoring charter schools remains controversial, feelings about pay for performance for teachers are also very divided. As with the goal of the No Child Left Behind law, it is difficult to argue with the idea that schools should be rewarding our best teachers. If we are to move forward in spreading this process, it would undoubtedly be helpful to know specifically how to introduce such a system successfully. The studies that have occurred thus far concerning the effectiveness of merit pay programs are not always helpful. Recently, a Texas plan, which spent $300 million on merit pay for teachers over a three-year period, concluded that the plan failed to have an impact on student achievement.[16]

While student achievement may not have improved, the same study showed that the incentive bonuses given to teachers positively affected teacher turn-over.[17] There have been a number of studies done in other countries. One in Portugal concluded that "overall, our results consistently indicate that the increased focus on individual teacher performance caused a sizeable and statistically significant decline in student achievement."[18]

At the same time, a "rigorous study" in India concluded that students of instructors who were receiving merit payments scored higher than teachers who were compensated through traditional pay structures.[19] Studies in Kenya and Israel had similar results. Even so, Thomas Toch of the *Detroit News* concluded in an editorial that it was a myth that merit pay had a "strong record."[20]

If one were to look at the evidence contained in studies to date, it is likely that he or she would agree with the conclusions of the Center for Public Education, which are as follows:

> Research on pay for performance plans, while still thin, suggests that performance-based pay can have a positive impact on student achievement, although the effects are relatively modest. However, there is little evidence about what type of rewards are most effective. And there is little long-term research to show whether these types of programs attract better-qualified individuals to teaching or keep them in the profession.

The same source noted that at least one "independent study found that the gains were obtained only in elementary schools.[21]

Another review of the research done on pay-for-performance systems suggests that there is no conclusive evidence to support or not to support such systems.[22] The fact is that almost every district and state that have experimented with such plans have created their own unique design. Still, it is also true that even without solid justification for pay for performance, one is hard pressed to defend the current method by which most teachers are paid. An *Education Week* article points out that 99 percent of tenured teachers in New York receive satisfactory ratings. Stephen Sawchuk compares the way we think of our tenured teachers to "the children in author Garrison Keillor's fictional town" where everyone is deemed "above average."[23]

The evaluation process and the method most often used to determine teachers' salaries have often come under attack. Lewis C. Solmon has written that "research shows that degrees, courses, and experiences that teachers have, beyond the first few years of teaching, are unrelated to how much their students achieve." He goes on to argue that "paying all teachers with the same experience and credits the same salary also ignores the fact that graduates of different fields have vastly different alternative career options; think of the physicist compared with someone having a bachelor's degree in elementary education."[24]

In his defense of the concept of pay for performance, Solmon highlights the Teacher Advancement Program in Madison, Arizona. The purpose of the program is to "attract, motivate, develop, and retain high-quality talent in the teaching profession." This program utilizes a number of approaches to merit pay. Included in the plan is the career ladder concept, a comprehensive evaluation system that includes "position responsibilities, classroom observations, and students' gains in test scores." The plan also provides professional growth opportunities "during the regular school day for teachers."[25]

One teacher education textbook takes the opposite view on merit pay for teachers. In the book *Teaching Today: An Introduction to Education,* the authors make the following argument:

Merit pay is based on the assumption that an individual only puts forth the minimum effort unless an incentive is provided to improve. This may well be the case in business where the goals of the employer and the employee are at odds. The goal of a business owner is to maximize production and profit while investing the least amount of resources. The goal of the employee is to maximize income with the least amount of effort. However, in teaching, the goals of the teacher and the organization are more closely aligned. For example, teachers learn that good teaching actually makes their job easier. If students are motivated and challenged, there is increased motivation and fewer discipline problems. Thus, good teaching has the reward of reducing teaching stress and effort. This is consistent with the district goal of providing a quality education. Therefore, increased incentives are not likely to significantly change teacher behavior.

In addition, for merit pay to work merit must be clearly defined and those in the merit pay system must accept that what is being rewarded is truly meritorious. There must be a clear answer to the question, "Why did X get merit pay?" If meritorious performance is not clearly defined, then the risk is that other variables such as personality and personal attractiveness become the basis for merit.[26]

Despite significant opposition to the concept, President Obama, even while he was recommending the elimination of funding for twelve federal education programs, included $517 million for performance pay grants in the proposed 2010 budget. In addition, his budget request also contained $200 million in the stimulus package for pay-for-performance programs. The guidelines for receiving this money include five core elements:

- Educating teachers and community about the plan
- Revising teacher- and principal-evaluation systems to guide classroom observations
- Providing professional development aligned to the new systems
- Linking student-achievement data to payroll systems
- Obtaining teacher, principal, and union support[27]

In preparing grants to establish new approaches to teacher compensation, the administration has consistently shared the conviction that any plans should be developed in cooperation with unions.[28]

Despite the opposition of teachers unions, the administration seems to have significant public and congressional support for merit pay for teachers. This is in spite of the fact that according to the Economic Policy Institute, "such plans are less common in the private sector than proponents claim." This report concluded that "only one in seven workers in the private sector is covered by bonus or merit-pay plans and most of those workers are in real-estate."[29]

Even if the practice is not widespread in other sectors of the economy, there is little question that there is an increased interest in our country in finding new ways to pay teachers. Perhaps the primary reason for this trend is that many have come to question the practice of paying teachers on a system based on years of service. While we are at least on the third or fourth wave of support for merit pay for teachers, there remains an inability to agree on a specific plan.[30]

Still, new ideas continue to emerge. In January of 2010, Georgia governor Sonny Perdue agreed to support legislation that would dramatically change the "statewide teacher-salary schedule and allow teachers to opt into one that determines pay partly on performance-based measures." No longer will those teachers who choose to enter the program receive supplements for advanced degrees, but rather would "win additional compensation based on observations of teachers and growth of student performance."[31]

Although the research that we have dealing with the success of such programs is less than totally conclusive, it might well be that with the support of public opinion, the administration, and a majority in Congress, the current movement "might not be as short-lived as in the past."[32]

Although pay-for-performance plans and charter schools remain quite controversial, a third priority of the Obama administration seems to have more widespread support. Since the inception of the Head Start program in 1965, the nation has increasingly involved its children in a variety of preschool or early childhood programs. This movement represents another major facet of the education program of Barack Obama.

NOTES

1. Johanna Sorrentino, "What's the Future of Merit Pay for Teachers?" Education.com, 2009, www.education.com/print/whats_the_future_merit_pay/ (accessed 2 December 2009).

2. Thomas Fitzgerald, "Obama Tells Teachers He Supports Merit Pay," Philly. com, 5 July 2007, www.philly.com/philly/news/8335627.html (accessed 1 September 2009).

3. Stephen Sawchuk, "NEA, Obama Administration May Not Be in Sync," *Education Week*, 7 July 2009, www.edweek.org/ew/articles/2009/07/07/36nea.h28.html &levelId=2100 (accessed 10 July 2009).

4. Ibid.

5. Ibid.

6. Ibid.

7. Beth Lewis, "Pros and Cons of Merit Pay for Teachers," About.com, k6educators .about.com/od/assessmentandtesting/a/meritpay.htm (accessed 2 December 2009).

8. Justin Snider, "Tying Teacher Tenure to Student Scores Doesn't Fly," *Education Week*, 9 February 2010, www.edweek.org/ew/articles/2010/02/10/21snider.h29 .html (accessed 10 February 2010).

9. Debra Viadero, "Study: Cash Not Needed to Motivate Competitive People," *Education Week*, 27 April 2010, blogs.edweek.org/edweek/inside-school research/2010/04/study_cash_not_needed_to_motiv.html (accessed 27 April 2010).

10. Arthea J. S. Reed, Verna E. Bergemann, Mary W. Olson, *In the Classroom: An Introduction to Education*, 3rd ed. (New York: McGraw-Hill, 1998), 29.

11. Meris Stansbury, "Teacher Quality under the Microscope," *eSchoolNews*, 20 August 2009, www.eschoolnews.com/news/top-news/news-by-subject/human resources/index.cfm . . . (accessed 2 December 2009).

12. Sam Dillon, "Long Reviled, Merit Pay Gains among Teachers," *New York Times*, 18 June 2007, www.nytimes.com/2007/06/18/education/18pay.html?_ r=1&pagewanted=print (accessed 2 December 2009).

13. Ibid.

14. "Survey Finds 'Gen Y' Teachers Open to Merit Pay," *Education Week*, 9 November 2009, www.edweek.org/ew/articles/2009/11/11/11report-b1.h29.html ?tkn=qpxf94j/d/5/ . . . (accessed 10 November 2009).

15. Ibid.

16. "Merit-Pay Study Finds Minimal Impact on Achievement," *Teacher Magazine*, 4 November 2009, www.edweek.org/tm/articles/2009/11/04/texasmeritpay_ap .html?tkn=pztf0rsh40 . . . (accessed 5 November 2009).

17. Debbie Viadero, "Texas Merit-Pay Failed to Boost Student Scores, Study Says," *Education Week*, 4 November 2009, blogs.edweek.org/edweek/inside-school-research/2009/11/texas_merit_pay_pilot_fail . . . (accessed 5 November 2009).

18. Mitchell Landsberg, "Study Pours Cold Water on Performance-Based Teacher Pay," *Los Angeles Times*, 18 September 2009, latimesblogs.latimes.com/lanow/ barack_obama/ (accessed 28 September 2009).

19. Debbie Viadero, "Whitehurts: Focus on Curriculum, Not Merit Pay, Charters," *Education Week*, 16 October 2009, blogs.edweek.org/edweek/inside-school research/2009/10/whitehurts.html (accessed 19 October 2009).

20. Thomas Toch, "Five Myths about Paying Good Teachers More," *Detroit News*, 13 October 2009, www.detnews.com.article/20091013/opinion01/910130314/1008/opinion01/five . . . (accessed 19 October 2009).

21. "Promise or Peril? Teacher Pay for Performace: At a Glance," *Center for Public Education*, 9 July 2009, www.centerforpubliceducation.org/site/apps/nlnet/content3.aspx?c=lvxin0jwe&b . . . (accessed 2 December 2009).

22. "Five Myths about Paying Good Teachers More."

23. Stephen Sawchuk, "Grade Inflation Seen in Evaluations of Teachers, Regardless of System," *Education Week*, 1 June 2009, www.edweek.org/ew/articles/2009/06/01/33evaluate.h28.html?tkn=luufshuwtdcf . . . (accessed 8 June 2009).

24. Lewis C. Solmon, "The Case for Merit Pay," in *Choice and Competition in American Education*, edited by Paul E. Peterson, (Lanham, Md.: Rowman & Littlefield, 2006), 102.

25. Ibid, 105.

26. David G. Armstrong, Kenneth T. Henson, Tom V. Savage, *Teaching Today: An Introduction to Education*, 8th ed. (Upper Saddle River, N.J.: Pearson, 2009), 365.

27. Stephen Sawchuk, "Dept. Unveils Revamped Rules for Teacher-Pay Fund," *Education Week*, 2 March 2010, www.edweek.org/ew/articles/2010/03/02/24tif.h29 .html (accessed 2 March 2010).

28. "Obama Tells Teachers He Supports Merit Pay."

29. Debbie Viadero, "Report Points to Risks of Merit Pay for Teachers," *Education Week*, 14 May 2009, www.edweek.org/login.html?source=www.edweek.org/ew/articles.2009/05/13 . . . (accessed 10 July 2009).

30. Stephen Sawchuk, "Ga. Governor Proposes Statewide Teacher-Pay Reform," *Education Week*, 15 January 2010, blogs.edweek.org/edweek/teacherbeat/2010/01/ga_governor_proposes_statewide.html (accessed 25 January 2010).

31. Ibid.

32. Debbie Viadero, "Teacher Compensation Ripe for Change, Author Says," *Education Week*, 13 October 2009, www.edweek.org/ew/articles/2009/10/14/07pay _ep.h29.html?tkn=rnofav0xntuc . . . (accessed 15 October 2009).

9

Early Childhood Education

Anne C. Lewis has written in *Phi Delta Kappan* that "the welfare of very young children was a federal concern through most of the last century in a fragmented way."[1] As early as 1912 under President William Howard Taft, Congress created the Children's Bureau "to investigate and report on all matters pertaining to the welfare of children."[2] As part of the New Deal during the Great Depression in the 1930s, the Public Works Administration established 1,500 preschools throughout the nation. It was estimated that 150,000 children benefited from such programs.[3]

An even larger program was developed as part of Lyndon Johnson's War on Poverty. Aimed at "disadvantaged children three to five years old," Head Start and, later, Early Head Start made available to communities large federal grants to establish comprehensive programs that focused not only on school readiness, but also on children's health and parental training.[4]

The issue emerged again in the 1970s when the Nixon administration recommended that early childhood education be added to the nation's priorities. Under the first President Bush, a National Education Summit led to the adoption of preschool education as a national priority by both the Education Commission of the States and the National Governors Association. The growth of interest resulted from studies showing that helping children to be well prepared to enter kindergarten would pay great dividends for the future academic success of many children.[5]

Still, federal funding for such programs has been inconsistent. In the final years of the administration of George W. Bush, appropriations for preschool education languished and even decreased. This was true despite the claim of one report that "high-quality preschool programs . . . could bring from $4 to $10 in future benefits for every dollar invested, largely because children with strong supports early in life do better in school and are more likely to be gainfully employed later."[6]

By 2002, even the mainstream media was talking about the value of early childhood programs. The well-known *Washington Post* columnist David Broder said in an editorial, "The evidence that high-quality education beginning at age 3 or 4 will pay lifetime dividends is overwhelming. The only question is whether we will make the needed investment."[7] Additional support became available with the publication of a major study in 2007 by the Graduate School of Education of the University of Pennsylvania which reported:

> The persistent achievement gaps among children of different race/ethnicity and socioeconomic status in the United States represent an issue that has commanded public, policy, and research attention on and off for about 100 years now, and it is once again in the forefront of policy-making agendas. Debates nevertheless abound on the most promising and cost-effective strategies to address the problem. We examine critically the available evidence on the benefits and cost of early childhood education and conclude that early vigorous interventions targeted at disadvantaged children offer the best chance to substantially reduce gaps in school readiness and increase the productivity of our educational systems.[8]

Gerald W. Bracey agreed when he pointed out that "ability gaps between the advantaged and disadvantaged open up early in the lives of children. Most of the gap, at age 18, is there at age 5."[9] Barack Obama undoubtedly has accepted this contention, both as a senator and as president. His proposals during the campaign included "a new program of Early Learning Challenge Grants, which would provide states with funding to support quality childcare, early education, and other services for pregnant women and children from birth through age five. States could use Early Learning Challenge Grant funds to support voluntary, high-quality preschool programs for three-and-four year olds."[10]

It should be noted that Obama was not suggesting mandatory preschool for all children, but rather that states be able to establish their own programs using federal funds. In addition, he called for the following steps:

- Quadruple Early Head Start: The Early Head Start program provides services to low-income children ages birth–3, and evaluations of the program have produced very positive findings. Early Head Start currently serves about 61,000 children.

- Increase Head Start Funding, which has stagnated under the Bush administration. The plan does not include specific targets for funding increases or numbers of additional youngsters served.
- Improve Head Start Quality: Provide $250 million to create or expand regional training centers to help Head Start centers implement successful models.
- Increase funding for the Child Care and Development Block Grant, which has stagnated under the Bush administration, resulting in the loss of services for 150,000 children. Obama would double quality funding within CCDBG, and would encourage states to use their quality set-aside funding to develop strategic plans that better coordinate all birth-to-five services.[11]

Later in the campaign, he would go even further in his support for early childhood education by suggesting that "we can start by investing $10 billion to guarantee access to quality, affordable, early childhood education for every child in America. Every dollar we spend on these programs puts our children on a path to success, while saving us as much as $10 in reduced health care cost, crime, and welfare later on."[12]

His published campaign literature also talked about "a preschool agenda that begins at birth." The campaign document went on to discuss one study that "shows that early experiences shape whether a child's brain develops strong skills for future learning, behavior, and success. Without a strong base on which to build, children, particularly disadvantaged children, will be behind long before they reach kindergarten."[13]

The comprehensive "Zero to Five" proposal by the Obama campaign would among other things "quadruple the number of eligible children for Early Head Start, increase Head Start funding, and improve quality for both." Obama's plan would also "work to ensure all children have access to preschool" and efforts would be made to "provide affordable and high-quality childcare that will ease the burden on working families." Finally, he proposed the creation of a "Presidential Early Learning Council" to ensure cooperation in implementing all of these programs "across federal, state, and local levels."[14]

It is clear from his speeches and campaign literature that Barack Obama, as a candidate, was committed to the expansion of federal action in the area of preschool education. The success of such an initiative is dependent on the support of Congress and the ability of the nation to provide necessary funding. Those most committed to the idea would have the federal government make it possible for all children to have necessary daycare and preschool opportunities.

In expanding the present system, one option is to have the public schools provide programs. Currently, most preschools and daycare facilities are privately operated. With the exception of Head Start and Early Head Start, they are funded by tuition paid by parents. This often includes programs offered by churches in their own buildings.

If the public schools are mandated to accept these children, there will undoubtedly be added expenses for teacher salaries. In addition, many districts will need to provide additional classrooms. On the other hand, if the majority of classes continue to be offered outside of the public schools, federal money paid to these programs will have to be monitored. The *Seattle Times* has suggested that efforts to regulate "early learning programs represent a vast no man's land with little in the way of standards or accountability. Teachers do not undergo background checks." In the state of Washington alone, there are 7,600 licensed child-care facilities that serve 175,000 children.[15]

If early childhood options were to expand, the regulatory problem would become even greater. This would also add to the need for public funds and could raise, in the case of church-sponsored programs, a constitutional issue. Short of a universal mandate is a program that makes preschool an option for parents. There are obviously parents who are doing an excellent job teaching their three- and four-year-olds at home. This is a conscious choice of these families and many would prefer to prepare their children for kindergarten themselves at home.

It is also possible that even if preschool programs were free to all families, one can still wonder if all of the parents whose children might benefit from early childhood education would take advantage of the opportunity. Of course, it could be made mandatory. Another approach is to continue to concentrate federal programs on disadvantaged children. If this is done it would mean dramatically expanding support of the Head Start and Early Head Start programs. Such an initiative would leave to state governments the role of increasing the options for families who are not eligible for the federal programs.

It is true that there is research that has supported the value of the Head Start program for poor children, but a new study has questioned the lasting effect of the benefits. An article in *Education Week* discusses a recent federal impact study that reported "Participation in Head Start has positive effects on children's learning while they're in the program, but most of the advantage they gain disappears by the end of first grade."[16]

The same study points out that there is a wide variety of quality in Head Start programs throughout the nation. In addition, the study reported on "only how Head Start children benefitted above and beyond children in other kinds of early-childhood settings." For the future, it was suggested that "exemplary programs should be identified and serve as models . . . but Head Start programs that are failing should be improved or terminated quickly to prevent serious harm to children."[17] The problems related to the future of early childhood education are not all involved with the question of how to expand opportunities.

Lillian Katz highlights the issue of the continuing conflict over appropriate preschool curriculum. She writes, "Disputes concerning curriculum and teaching methods go back a long way in the field of early childhood education."[18] A number of educators emphasize the need to prepare children to succeed in language arts and math. With the requirement for mandatory tests in these areas as a result of the No Child Left Behind law, schools are tempted to emphasize academic skills in their preschool programs.

The law itself promotes the use of Early Reading First programs. This is being done despite the fact that it has been suggested that the program's "effectiveness is illusive" and "unimpressive." It has also been noted that the Early Reading First curriculum for preschool children is expensive. One source claimed that it cost $80,000 per year to finance its use in a single classroom.[19]

On the other side of the debate there have always been those who see the primary benefit of early education as being social. This argument was highlighted in a *Washington Post* article titled "The Playtime's the Thing." The author points to research showing that by age twenty-three, "people who attended play-based preschools were eight times less likely to need treatment for emotional disturbances than those who went to preschools where direct instruction prevailed."[20]

Emma Brown, the author of the article, noted that the same study demonstrates that "graduates of the play-based preschools were three times less likely to be arrested for committing a felony." She referred to other research reporting that these types of programs "have a measureable effect on children's ability to control their impulses. That skill is more closely correlated to academic success in kindergarten than intelligence is."[21] It is likely that the Obama administration and most educators will agree to the need for both academic and social experiences in preschool education, but undoubtedly the curriculum debate will continue.

Even though the first years of the Obama administration have been primarily concerned with foreign policy, the economy, and health care, the president has not neglected his support for early childhood education. In a speech to the United States Hispanic Chamber of Commerce on March 10, 2009, he listed his five pillars for educational reform. The first one listed was "investing in early childhood initiatives like Head Start."[22]

In September of 2009, *Education Week* reported that even "amid a recession that's squeezing state budgets and pushing more families into poverty, teams of officials from 39 states gathered near Washington this week to explore ways to better meet the educational and health needs of young children." It is noted that Congress and the president in their initiatives to stimulate the economy in the American Recovery and Reinvestment Act provided at least $5 billion for early childhood education.[23]

Beyond that, the *New York Times* reported in September of 2009 that "tucked away in an $87 billion higher education bill that passed the House last week was a broad new federal initiative aimed not at benefiting college students, but raising the quality in the early learning and care programs that serve children from birth through age five."[24]

It was expected that the Senate would agree and that the legislation would be ready for the president's signature in December. Unfortunately, while the federal government was increasing funding for preschool programs, there was concern that because of the recession states might reduce their spending. At least as of the fall of 2009, "thirty states had already decided to maintain or even add to their preschool budgets."[25]

Still, in April of 2010, there were those who were disappointed by the possible lack of commitment of the Obama administration to early childhood education. An article by Linda Jacobson pointed to the fact that during the recent amending of the student loan program, there was no money included for the president's proposed Early Learning Challenge Fund, "which would have provided competitive grants to help states create and improve the quality of services for at-risk children from birth to age five." While advocates of early childhood education were disappointed in this lack of funding, they have already begun to lobby for new allocations as part of the reauthorization of the No Child Left Behind law.[26]

Despite the concerns of the supporters of early childhood education, Secretary of Education Duncan has consistently supported such programs. In December of 2009, he highlighted the importance of the federal government's role in encouraging programs for young children. In a meeting at which he shared the podium with the U.S. Secretary of Health and Human Services, Kathleen Sebelius, Duncan pointed out that "we're trying to get out of the catch-up business." Both cabinet members during their presentation highlighted the connection between their departmental programs. Sebelius was quoted as saying, "You can't learn unless you are healthy." She also emphasized that we have "a president who gets the importance of a strong preschool education."[27]

Even with the strong support of the president and Secretary Duncan, the question of additional federal and state support for preschool education will be significantly affected by what happens to our national economy during the next several years. The stimulus package aid is now scheduled for only two years, unless additional funds are made available after that. In addition, the results of the midterm election in 2010 could affect any decision concerning future funding. There is no question that there is a rising concern about the increase of the federal deficit. Republicans, especially, may be unwilling to support measures that are funded by additional borrowing.

Still, there can be little question that Barack Obama remains committed to federal assistance for preschool education programs, especially those being provided for underprivileged children. It is safe to predict that this area of educational spending will continue to be a priority for his administration. While this is likely, there remains the serious need for additional research and policy discussions that will "precisely identify" the "features of preschool programs with the greatest benefits for children."

Although the results of the research in this area are mixed, a recent study in the city of Los Angeles has reaffirmed the benefits of preschool education. The *Los Angeles Times* reported in April of 2010 that "children enrolled in Los Angeles Universal Preschool programs have made significant improvements in the social and emotional skills needed to do well in kindergarten."[28]

In addition, there is the need to create professional development opportunities for the adults responsible for providing these programs. Finally, the government must establish ways to monitor the use of federal government funds that are being made available to states and local communities.[29] If these challenges can be met, there is good reason to believe that an increased emphasis on preschool education will be a positive way for improving the academic performance of our nation's children.

NOTES

1. Anne C. Lewis, "Adding Young Children to the Federal Agenda," *Phi Delta Kappan*, March 2009, 459.

2. Ruth Wood Gavian and William A. Hamm, *United States History* (Boston: Heath, 1960), 541–42.

3. L. Dean Webb, *The History of American Education* (Upper Saddle River, N.J.: Pearson, 2006), 250.

4. Ibid., 288.

5. Anne C. Lewis, "Adding Young Children to the Federal Agenda," *Washington Commentary*, March 2009, 459.

6. Ibid.

7. Gerald W. Bracey, "Investing in Preschool," in *Charting a Professional Course*, ed. Don Kauchak, Paul Eggen, and Mary D. Burbank, (Upper Saddle River, N.J.: Pearson, 2004), 63.

8. Irma Perez-Johnson and Rebecca Maynard, "The Case for Early, Targeted Interventions to Prevent Academic Failure," *Peabody Journal of Education*, 2007, 587.

9. Gerald W. Bracey, "An Ounce of Prevention," *Phi Delta Kappan*, November 2008, 225.

10. Sara Mead, "Primary Watch: Barack Obama's Early Education Agenda," *New America Foundation*, 10 April 2008, www.newamerica.net/blog/early-ed -watch/2008/primary-watch-barack-obamas-early-education-agenda-3239 (accessed 1 September 2009).

11. Ibid.

12. Sara Mead, "Campaign Watch: Barack Obama Links Early Ed to America's Economic Well-Being," *New America Foundation*, 18 June 2008, www.newamerica.net/ blog/early-ed-watch/2008/campaign-watch-barack-obama-links-early-ed-americas -economic-well-being-4603 (accessed 28 September 2009).

13. "Barack Obama's Plan for Lifetime Success through Education," *Obama'08*, www.barackobama.com (accessed 12 October 2009).

14. Ibid.

15. "Early Start on Early Learning," *Seattle Times*, 19 January 2010, seattletimes .nwsource.com/html/editorials/2010835197_edit20preschool.html (accessed 22 January 2010).

16. Mary Ann Zehr, "Head Start Study Finds Brief Learning Gains," *Education Week*, 14 January 2010, www.edweek.org/ew/articles/2010/01/14/18headstart.h29. html (accessed 19 January 2010).

17. Ibid.

18. Lillian Katz, "Curriculum Disputes in Early Childhood Education," *ERIC Digest*, University of Illinois, December 1999.

19. Mary Ann Zehr, "Literacy Bill Includes Pieces of Federal Program," *Education Week*, 7 December 2009, www.edweek.org/login.html?source=www.edweek.org/ ew/articles/2009/12/09/14read_ep.h29.html&destination=www.edweek.org/ew/ articles/2009/12/09/14read_ep.h29.html&levelId=2100 (accessed 8 December 2009).

20. Emma Brown, "The Playtime's the Thing," *Washington Post*, 21 November 2009, www.washingtonpost.com/wp-dyn/content/article/2009/11/20/AR2009112002391 .html (accessed 23 November 2009).

21. Ibid.

22. "White House Reports on a Speech by President Obama to U.S. Hispanic Chamber of Commerce, March 10, 2009," www.whitehouse.gov, 10 March 2009, www.eddigest.com (accessed 6 January 2010).

23. Erik W. Robelen, "Early Education Issues Return to Spotlight," *Education Week*, 18 September 2009, www.edweek.org/login.html?source=www.edweek.org/ ew/articles/2009/09/18/04nga-early.h29.html&destination=www.edweek.org/ew/ articles/2009/09/18/04nga-early.h29.html&levelId=2100 (accessed 18 September 2009).

24. Sam Dillon, "Initiative Focuses on Early Learning Programs," *New York Times*, 19 September 2009, www.nytimes.com/2009/09/20/education/20child.html (accessed 21 September 2009).

25. Ibid.

26. Linda Jacobson, "Advocates Weigh Obama's Commitment to Early Ed," *Education Week*, 12 April 2010, www.edweek.org/ew/articles/2010/04/09/29obama -earlyed_ep.h29.html (accessed 13 April 2010).

27. Mary Ann Zehr, "Duncan: Preschool Will Help Country 'Get Out of the Catch-Up Business,'" *Education Week*, 8 December 2009, blogs.edweek.org/edweek/curric ulum/2009/12/arne_duncan_were_trying_to_get.html (accessed 9 December 2009).

28. Carla Rivera, "L.A. Study Affirms Benefits of Preschool," *Los Angeles Times*, 19 April 2010, www.latimes.com/news/local/la-me-0420-preschool -20100419,0,2289045.story (accessed 20 April 2010).

29. Laura M. Justice and Carol Vukelich, *Achieving Excellence in Preschool Literacy Instruction* (New York: Guilford Press, 2008), 19–20.

10

The National Standards Movement

The word *standards* has a number of meanings in the English language. In the field of education, we most often use the word in reference to measurable goals. We have talked about setting high standards for our students. During the past several decades, educators have begun to speak and write about curriculum standards in a different way. A new definition has emerged that refers to curriculum standards as what students should know and be able to do in a specific curriculum area. Since the 1980s, states and school districts have been engaged in attempting to define specifically what students should be learning in the major academic areas of the curriculum.

In some cases, the standards that have been written are very general and allow schools and teachers considerable latitude in what and how they teach. Other states have gone in the opposite direction and have created extended documents containing the specific information and skills that must be taught. As part of the standards movement, assessments have been developed to measure how well the students have mastered the knowledge and skills included in the curriculum standards.

Increasingly, the results of these tests or assessments have been used to measure the effectiveness of our schools. The new accountability, which has emerged as a result of what we now call "high-stakes testing," has had significant impact on what is occurring in classrooms throughout the nation. The standards movement, high-stakes testing, and increased accountability can be traced back to a report written during the presidency of Ronald Reagan. Even though the Republican Party appeared to have little use for the federal Department of Education, President Reagan's Secretary of Education, Terrel Bell, decided to initiate an educational review process at the national level.[1]

He did so by appointing a group of educators and representatives of business and higher education to what was called the National Commission on Excellence in Education. The group began its work in August of 1981, and for a year and a half these volunteers, along with a full-time staff, held hearings and gathered data. In April of 1983, they submitted their report to Secretary Bell and the president.[2]

Their findings were included in a document titled *The Nation at Risk Report*. Its stirring introduction was highly publicized throughout the nation:

> Our nation is at risk. Our once unchallenged prominence in commerce, industry, science, and technological innovation is being overtaken by competitors throughout the world. . . . If an unfriendly foreign power had attempted to impose on America the mediocre educational performance that exists today, we might well have viewed it as an act of war. As it stands, we have allowed this to happen to ourselves. We have even squandered the gains in student achievement made in the wake of the Sputnik challenge. Moreover, we have dismantled essential support systems, which helped make those gains possible. We have, in effect, been committing an act of unthinking, unilateral educational disarmament.[3]

The report concentrated primarily on high schools and charged that the curriculum of our schools had become "homogenized, diluted, and diffused."[4] The implication of such criticisms seemed to make clear the need to create more rigorous curriculum requirements, as well as examinations that would assess students' mastery of the content and skills required by the curriculum. The report gave examples of what the authors considered excellent standards in each academic area. For example, in science they argued that the following should be included:

- The concepts, laws, and processes of the physical and biological sciences
- The methods of scientific inquiry and reasoning
- The application of scientific and technological development
- The social and environmental implications of scientific and technological development[5]

For social studies, they suggested these objectives:

- Enable students to fix their places and possibilities within the larger social and cultural structure
- Understand the broad sweep of both ancient and contemporary ideas that have shaped our world

- Understand the fundamentals of how our economic system works and how our political system functions
- Grasp the difference between free and repressive societies[6]

Among the results of the report was a movement at the state level to identify curriculum standards, especially in language arts, math, social studies, and science. While the standards movement began at the state level, by 1989 Albert Shanker, president of the American Federation of Teachers, in a speech to the Governors Conference, would call for a national system of standards and assessment.[7]

Bill Clinton, who presided over that meeting, upon his election as president instructed the Department of Education to appoint a commission to develop voluntary curriculum standards in several curriculum areas. Meanwhile, Congress was also interested in standards, and when the Republican Party gained majority control in 1994, the process of creating standards was delegated to the states.[8] A national education summit in 1996, which included both governors and business leaders, helped promote the development of state curriculum standards. By the year 2000, forty-nine states had developed their own standards.[9]

Here is an example of a skills-based standard (Georgia standards, grade 7, social studies skills):

The student should 1) Locate main ideas in multiple types of sources (e.g., non-print, specialized references, periodicals, newspapers, atlases, yearbooks, government publications, etc.). 2) Take notes and develop outlines through reading, listening, or viewing. 3) Use features of books for information: table of contents, glossary, index, appendix, bibliography. 4) Distinguish between fact and opinion relating to regions/cultures.[10]

This is a sample of a knowledge-based standard (California standards, standard 3, grade 10):

The student will identify the sources and describe the development of democratic principles in Western Europe and the United States. . . . After examining major documents (such as the Declaration of Independence, the Constitution of the United States, the English Bill of Rights, the Declaration of the Rights of Man, or the Universal Declaration of Human Rights) for the specific democratic principles they contain, the student makes a comparison chart showing how certain principles appear in these documents.[11]

Early in the decade of the 1990s, the idea of creating national education goals and standards was a topic of serious consideration. A document titled

"Goals 2000" introduced the idea of national standards as a way to ensure success in achieving the goals that were established.[12] When No Child Left Behind was being debated, there was some sentiment in Congress for creating national curriculum standards and testing. In the end, it was decided to continue to allow the states to determine curriculum and to develop appropriate tests.

At the same time, there were provisions in the law that were meant to help the federal government hold states and schools accountable. State standards and tests were to be approved by the federal government. While most states already had developed their own assessment program, No Child Left Behind mandated that every state develop examinations in language arts and math for students in grades 3–8, and science tests that would be required at the elementary, middle school, and high school level.

The law had strong bipartisan support, and President Bush was hopeful that it would become one of the major accomplishments of his presidency. Initially, public support for the law was strong, although there were many, including a significant number of teachers, who were concerned about a number of the provisions. Supporters pointed to the failures of progressive education methods and believed that there was a need to "go back to basics." In his book *Cultural Literacy*, author E. D. Hersh argued:

> The common knowledge characteristically shared by those at the top of the socioeconomic ladder in the United States should be readily available to all citizens because people who lack it suffer serious handicaps. This "core knowledge" is needed for productive communication and establishing fundamental equality as citizens. That is the content of basic education and should be the primary focus of schooling.[13]

On the other hand, critics of the law would agree with Theodore S. Sizer, who wrote in his book *Horace's Compromise* that "'machine-scored standardized tests would not solve our education problems."[14] Increasingly, the law has been criticized because it has narrowed the curriculum by causing schools to spend more time on those areas where testing is mandated and less time on other aspects of the curriculum. The increased emphasis on testing and accountability has also created the feeling among many that teachers are being forced to "teach to the test."

Although it was scheduled to be reauthorized in 2007, Congress has been slow to act. Because of provisions in the original legislation, No Child Left Behind will stay in effect as written or amended until it is reauthorized. Among the issues to be resolved is whether or not the present state curriculum standards and tests should be replaced by those created at the national level. The arguments on both sides of this debate are for the most part unchanged from what they were during the Clinton administration, except that we now have a history of state standards and assessments to consider. Those on the side of continued state control have both the U.S. Constitution and history on their side. Because the Constitution does not include education as a delegated power for the national government, it was considered for much of our history as an area reserved for the states. Even though this was an accepted principle for many years, the federal government has become involved in the field of education increasingly during the twentieth century. The major initiative came as part of President Johnson's War on Poverty. In 1965, the Elementary Secondary Education Act, which later became No Child Left Behind, included not only vast amounts of money for schools, but also regulations on how it should be spent.

Conservatives, including President Ronald Reagan, have not been friendly to legislation placing the government in Washington in a position to regulate how our schools are to function. The Republican Party has actually included in their party platform a plank calling for the abolition of a separate federal Department of Education. As the movement for the establishment of national curriculum standards continues, one can expect to hear from critics who would agree with President Reagan when he said, "The federal government does not solve problems, it is the problem." This sentiment, however, is not one that is necessarily shared by a majority of our citizens.

Proponents of the creation of common standards now point to the fact that academic expectations vary greatly from one state to another. As a result, even some prominent Republicans, including the former secretaries of education William Bennett and Rod Paige, have publicly called for replacing the state standards with uniform federal curriculums and tests.[15]

In an article in the *Washington Post* in September of 2006, Paige and Bennett cited statistics showing that while Tennessee reported on its state test "eighty-seven percent of its fourth-graders are proficient in reading, the results for students in Tennessee on the National Assessment of Educational Progress Tests set the number at twenty-seven percent." In addition, the article referred to Oklahoma, where they charge that bureaucrats in the state education department had lowered the passing standards of their tests to ensure that their scores would show "Adequate Yearly Progress" under No Child Left Behind.[16]

A similar concern can be seen in a comment of Barack Obama quoted in the March 14, 2009, issue of *The Economist*. "Mr. Obama lamented, fourth-grade (i.e., nine-year-old) readers in Mississippi can score seventy points worse than their peers in Wyoming and receive the same grade." The president goes on to note that with "no central control of standards, states can get free money simply by making tests easier to pass."[17]

Barack Obama is not the only one who has been worrying about the difference in the academic expectations of the states. In an article in the *Washington Post* in February of 2009, American Federation of Teachers president Randi Weingarten was quoted as saying, "Abundant evidence suggests that common, rigorous standards lead to more students reaching higher levels of achievement. The countries that consistently outperform the United States on international assessments all have national standards, with core curriculum, assessments and time for professional development for teachers based on those standards."[18]

Added impetus for the immediate creation of national standards came just two months after President Obama took office. It was at the Governors Conference in 2009 that a process was endorsed to begin work on national curriculum standards. In doing so, the governors were joining with the Council of the Great City Schools, the National Association of Secondary School Principals, and the American Federation of Teachers in endorsing "the idea that the nation set a common definition of what students should know and be able to do."[19]

Secretary Duncan quickly responded to this movement by commenting on what the appropriate federal role should be in regard to this initiative. In an interview on C-SPAN, he said, "We want to get into this game" . . . but "I'm not leading this game."[20] By April of 2009, even *Time* was praising the movement for national standards. Walter Isaacson charged that our schools are "burdened by an incoherent jumble of state and local curriculum standards, assessment tools, tests, texts and teaching materials. Even worse, many states have bumbled into a race to the bottom as they define their local standards downward in order to pretend to satisfy federal demands by showing that their students are proficient."[21]

In the same month, representatives of forty-one states came together in Chicago for what was hoped to be "a first, concrete step toward common guidelines in mathematics and English-language arts."[22] As the process began, it was thought that language arts and math might be the easiest subjects in which to reach agreement but, as might be expected, there have been disagreements. With language arts, the debate has centered on "whether to focus on decoding and basic skills or to develop reading habits." Those working on the math standards have debated "whether to emphasize algorithms or conceptual knowledge."[23]

Even with these potential sticking points, support for national standards continues to grow. In an article published in *USA Today* in June 2009, several new arguments were put forward. It was suggested that "standards will save states money. They collectively spend more than \$1 billion developing and administering 50 different tests, so having a uniform assessment should cut millions in cost." The same article pointed out that common standards will "ease the transition for students who move from one state to another."[24]

Negative publicity for the current state tests is also helping gain public support for a national takeover. In a 2009 study that included forty-seven states, the researchers concluded, "Various states made their standards less rigorous in one or more grade levels or subjects in at least twenty-six instances."[25] These actions were most probably taken so that states could avoid having so many of their schools being labeled as "in need of improvement" under the provisions of No Child Left Behind.

Editorial support for state involvement in the national standards movement was also evident. For example, the *St. Petersburg Times* began an editorial by noting that "Florida has joined a smart national movement in education. It is one of forty-six states that have just agreed to develop uniform national standards." The same editorial pointed out that the federal government had allotted $350 million to assist the movement that is seeking to create common standards and assessments.[26]

Although his support listed several precautions for the movement, Jack Jennings wrote in the *American School Board Journal* in September of 2009 that "our curriculum for eighth-graders is two full years behind top-performing countries. That's a prescription for economic decline. . . . Arguments for national standards are persuasive. Reading and math, the subjects most discussed, are fields of knowledge where we should have national agreement." While supporting the concept, Jennings raises a number of questions that must be dealt with:

- Who decides on the academic content?
- Who determines which tests are to be used?
- Who sets the proper cutoff score? Is it the federal government; the governors as a group; or some combination of governors, businesspeople, state school superintendents, and educators?
- Who supports such a group?
- How can you form a creditable group that represents a variety of opinions about academic subjects and types of tests, and still have agreements reached?[27]

In the same article, Jennings advises the Obama administration to allow the common standards movement to be the work of "the state governors, state school superintendents, and others. Let them take the lead and flesh out the details of how to achieve a heightening of rigor in the public schools."[28]

In July of 2009, a commentary in *Education Week* joined the chorus of support for the movement. Quentin Suffren wrote:

> More than seven years into the No Child Left Behind era, it's become painfully evident that there are numerous interpretations of "accountability" across just as many states (a recent report from the Thomas B. Fordham Institute, "The Accountability Illusion" sizes this up well). At the core of this inconsistency are the almost fifty sets of state content standards, many of which are mediocre in quality, that mandate course expectations for kindergarten through grade 12. These standards serve as the foundation for course curricula, but in too many states they are capricious, bloated and unwieldy.[29]

In October of 2009, the *Boston Globe* added its support for the movement. Noting that forty-eight states were now committed to the project, the editorial quoted Education Secretary Arne Duncan as saying, "We're lying to our children when we tell them they're proficient."[30] A month later, the National Parent Teachers Association, with more than five million members, also published an article in their monthly magazine endorsing the national movement for creating standards. Sean Cavanagh, the author of the article, also pointed to the fact that the Gates Foundation was contributing funding for the movement.[31]

While it would seem that momentum for creating national standards was increasing, the opposition to the concept could also be heard. In a book of essays titled *Education and the Making of a Democratic People,* Paul G. Theobald was critical of the entire standards movement. In writing about the "dark side" of standard-based reform, he quotes "Yale's well-known creativity expert, Robert Sternberg, as saying: 'The increasingly massive and far-reaching use of conventional standardized tests is one of the most effective, if unintentional, vehicles this country has created for suppressing creativity.'"[32]

Marion Brady, in an article in *Education Week,* also expressed concern about the standards movement. For her, at least, it is a curriculum that

> disregards research and common sense about the contributions of art, music, dance, and play to intellectual development; overworks short-term memory to the neglect of all other cognitive processes; costs an appalling amount to administer; doesn't progress smoothly through ever-increasing levels of intellectual complexity; and is keyed not to learners' attitudes, abilities, and interests, but to their ages; . . . fails to explore questions essential to ethical and moral development; emphasizes minimum standards rather than maximum performance; and snubs major sources of America's past strength and success—individual initiative, imagination, and creativity.[33]

She goes on to predict:

If implemented as it's being advocated by spokespersons, the national standards–reform effort will fail. Period. It won't fail because subject-matter specialists can't agree on standards. And it won't fail because of teacher incompetence, weak administrators, "the soft bigotry of low expectations," union resistance to change, parental indifference, inadequate funding, lack of rigor, failure to employ market forces, too few charter schools, too little technology, or any other currently popular explanations of poor performance.

It will fail for the same reason the No Child Left Behind Act failed—because it will be driven by data derived from simplistic tests keyed to simplistic standards, keyed to a simplistic, dysfunctional, obsolete, 19th century curriculum.[34]

Despite such dire warnings by what some would call "progressive educators," the process of developing national standards continues. The pressure for adopting the common standards has intensified as the administration has now made it mandatory for states to agree that they will accept the new standards in order to receive a Race to the Top grant.[35] Once they are adopted, most observers agree that this will be followed by instituting a system of national tests.

Such a result will not be unique to the United States; many, if not most, developed nations have national testing programs. There will undoubtedly be problems agreeing on these standards and tests, especially in subjects such as social studies. In addition, concerns have been expressed about possible conflicts of interest that might arise during the process. It has been noted that some of the people who are involved in creating common standards are "representatives of multiple commercial entities that stand to profit enormously from selling curricula, instructional materials, assessments, and consultancies as the standards are rolled out."[36]

When in early March 2010, after a year of work, a new draft of language arts and math standards was made public, the reaction was mixed. In regard to language arts, a difference emerged between those who feel that the draft requires "skills such as critical thinking without the underlying subject-matter knowledge required to learn those skills." Richard Long believes that "too much focus on subject-matter in standards, . . . risks turning schooling into a mechanical use of facts, rather than a process of learning how to apply key skills to varying sets of facts."[37]

There was also some concern over the draft of the math standards. Henry S. Kepner Jr., president of the National Council of Teachers of Mathematics, supported the fact that there is an emphasis on "problem-solving" and "reasoning," but he believes that these skills "are not evident enough throughout the document."[38]

Because of some of the questions being raised, it is unlikely that (per the president's prediction) in early 2010, we will have a finished document that could be adopted by the states.[39] Obtaining voluntary state approval of uniform curriculum standards and tests will not happen quickly. Doing so is an extremely complicated and controversial process that will need the support, not only of the states and the Congress, but also hopefully, of all of the interest groups involved in the educational process. Should the Obama administration be successful in creating national curriculum standards and testing, it will be a revolutionary change in the field of public education.

During the evolvement of the standards movement, "one of its key questions has shifted. Instead of simply asking what students should know and be able to do to complete high school, educators and policy makers are now asking what students need to master to be prepared for the higher-level demands of college and career."[40] This concern about higher education is another initiative that is important to Barack Obama.

NOTES

1. William Hayes, *Are We Still a Nation at Risk Two Decades Later?* (Lanham, Md.: Scarecrow Education, 2004), 11–19.

2. Ibid.

3. Myra Pollack Sadker and David Miller Sadker, *Teachers, Schools, and Society*, 5th ed. (New York: McGraw-Hill, 2000), 148–49.

4. U.S. Department of Education, National Commission on Excellence in Education, *A Nation at Risk: The Imperative for Educational Reform*, April 1983, Introduction, 8.

5. Ibid., 2.

6. Ibid.

7. Peter S. Hlebowitsh, *Foundations of American Education* (Toronto: Wadsworth, 2001), 543–44.

8. Ibid.

9. Myra Pollack Sadker and David Miller Sadker, *Teachers, Schools, and Society*, 6th ed. (New York: McGraw-Hill, 2003), 272.

10. *Foundations of American Education*, 550.

11. Ibid.

12. Ibid., 544–45.

13. Jack L. Nelson, Stuart B. Palonsky, and Mary Rose McCarthy, *Critical Issues in Education: Dialogues and Dialectics* (New York: McGraw-Hill, 2004), 235.

14. Diane Ravitch, *Left Back: A Century of Battles over School Reform* (New York: Touchstone, 2000), 418.

15. William J. Bennett and Rod Paige, "Why We Need a National School Test," *Washington Post*, 21 September 2006.

16. Ibid.

17. "The Teacher-in-Chief Speaks: Barack Obama and Education," *The Economist*, 14 March 2009.

18. Randi Weingarten, "The Case for National Standards," *Washington Post*, 16 February 2009.

19. David J. Hoff, "National Standards Gain Steam," *Education Week*, 2 March 2009, www.edweek.org/ew/articles/2009/03/04/23nga_ep.h28.html?tmp=1877370801 (accessed 4 March 2009).

20. Ibid.

21. Walter Isaacson, "How to Raise the Standard in America's Schools," *Time*, 25 April 2009, www.time.com/time/nation/article/0,85599,1891468,00.html (accessed 27 April 2009).

22. Michele McNeil, "NGA, CCSSO Launch Common Standards Drive," *Education Week*, 17 April 2009, www.edweek.org/ew/articles/2009/04/16/29standards.h28.html (accessed 22 April 2009).

23. Zach Miners, "Support Builds for National Standards," *District Administration*, 12 April 2009.

24. Ledyard King, "46 States to Toughen Standards," *USA Today*, 2 June 2009.

25. Debra Viadero, "NCES Finds States Lowered 'Proficiency' Bar," *Education Week*, 29 October 2009, www.edweek.org/ew/articles/2009/10/29/10nces.h29.html (accessed 29 October 2009).

26. "Raising the Bar for Our Schools," *St. Petersburg Times*, 16 June 2009.

27. Jack Jennings, "National Standards," *American School Board Journal*, September 2009.

28. Ibid.

29. Quentin Suffren, "The Death of Quality by Consensus," *Education Week*, 21 July 2009, www.edweek.org/ew/articles/2009/07/21/37suffren.h28.html (accessed 27 July 2009).

30. Libby Quaid, "Many States Set Low Bar on Student Proficiency; Report Cites Wide Range in Standards," *Boston Globe*, 30 October 2009.

31. Sean Cavanagh, "PTA Launches Campaign Backing Common Standards," *Education Week*, 1 December 2009, www.edweek.org/ew/articles/ 2009/12/01/14pta.h29.html (accessed 2 December 2009).

32. John I. Goodlad, Roger Soder, and Bonnie McDaniel (eds.), *Education and the Making of Democratic People* (Boulder, Colo.: Paradigm Publishers, 2008), 74.

33. Marion Brady, "National Subject-Matter Standards? Be Careful What You Wish For," *Education Week*, 22 September 2009, www.edweek.org/ew/articles/2009/09/23/04brady.h29.html (accessed 24 September 2009).

34. Ibid.

35. Catherine Gewerts, "Seeking an End to the 'Massachusetts Madness,'" *Education Week*, 25 May 2010, blogs.edweek.org/edweek/curriculum/2010/05/seeking_an_end_to_the_massachu.html (accessed 26 May 2010).

36. Mary Ann Zehr, "Conflict of Interest Arises as Concern in Standards Push," *Education Week*, 2 November 2009, www.edweek.org/ew/articles/2009/11/04/10conflict_ep.h29.html (accessed 2 November 2009).

37. Catherine Gewertz, "Draft Common Standards Elicit Kudos and Criticism," *Education Week*, 10 March 2010, www.edweek.org/ew/articles/2010/03/10/25common _ep.h29.html (accessed 12 March 2010).

38. Ibid.

39. "Prepared Remarks of President Barack Obama at a 'Race to the Top' Announcement; Location: Madison, Wisconsin," *Federal News Service*, 4 November 2009.

40. Catherine Gewertz, "College and the Workforce: What 'Readiness' Means," *Education Week*, 14 January 2010, www.edweek.org/ew/articles/2010/01/14/17readiness .h29.html (accessed 15 January 2010).

11

The Initiatives in Higher Education
and Teacher Education

The same week that Barack Obama took office as president of the United States, *University World News* published an article titled "Obama and Higher Education: Promises and Problems." It identified the president's goals for higher education as improving the student loan program, increasing access to higher education, providing tax credits for college expenses, and aiding community colleges with a focus on technical education. In addition, it mentioned the administration's plan to support "affirmative action to close the economic and educational gaps some minorities experience." In seeking this objective, the president has made it clear that such affirmative action programs should "take into account class as well as race factors."[1]

During its first year in office, the Obama administration was very active in attempting to carry out a number of these objectives.

- In February 2009, Congress passed and the president signed into law a continuation of the 2009 budget, which increased the Pell maximum grant by $119 from $5,231 to $5,350 beginning in academic year 2009. In the president's 2010 submission, the Pell grant was increased to $5,550, and he suggested increases tied to the Consumer Price Index beginning in 2011.
- The American Recovery and Reinvestment Act (the stimulus bill), signed into law by President Obama in February 2009, includes a provision for a tax credit of up to $2,500 of college expenses, including tuition, fees, and course materials. Up to 40 percent ($1,000) is refundable, meaning that those who do not owe on their taxes could receive the credit in the form of a rebate.

- Included in the American Recovery and Reinvestment Act, the State Fiscal Stabilization Fund provides funds to states to make up for spending reductions as a result of the economy, specifically for education, including postsecondary education. For the fiscal years 2009, 2010, and 2011, approximately $48.6 billion will be available to governors to assist in restoring depleted state accounts for higher education and elementary and secondary education.
- Additional funds from the State Fiscal Stabilization Fund have been made available to be used for the modernization, repair, or renovation of school and college buildings.
- The American Recovery and Reinvestment Act also includes $100 million for the Teacher Quality Enhancement Program. Some of this money will be available to colleges that provide teacher education programs.[2]

All of these things were accomplished during the first year of the Obama presidency.

In March of 2009, the president reiterated his commitment to higher education when he listed it as one of the five pillars of educational reform. He is in favor of "providing every American with higher education whether it's college or technical training."[3] In a speech a month later, Obama spoke about a "paradox of American life." He described it this way: "At the very moment that it's never been more important to have a quality higher education, the cost of that kind of education has never been higher." Pointing to the dramatic increases in tuition, he noted that family incomes have not come near to keeping up with the cost of a college education. In response to this, he pointed to the administration's success in providing a $2,500 annual tax credit to help pay for tuition costs.[4]

Because so many college students have accumulated large debts to pay for their education, in January of 2010 the Obama administration "proposed expanding a popular program that caps monthly student loan payments for college graduates with low or moderate income. . . . Under the proposal, monthly payments on federal loans would be limited to 10 percent of discretionary income—above a 'basic living allowance'—for qualified borrowers."[5]

At the same time, the Education Department was working on a plan to revise the form used by students seeking federal aid to help finance their college education. *Education Week* reported progress with this initiative, noting that "high school seniors who used a highly simplified version of the daunting federal application for student financial aid [Free Application for Federal Student Aid, or FAFSA]—and had help completing it—were 30 percent more likely to enroll in college the next fall than were their peers who had no such assistance." This was just a trial run for the revised form.[6]

By January of 2010, the new version of FAFSA was being used by the twenty million students seeking aid for the coming year. Concerning the form, "officials provided an example of a hypothetical 17-year-old who receives a reduced-price lunch at school, is not employed, plans to attend college in the fall, and lives with two parents who report an adjusted gross income of $45,000." Such a student will answer twenty-two fewer questions than on the previous form. At the same time, the Education Department is also attempting to develop a system that would "allow tax-return information to be downloaded straight onto the aid application."[7]

As part of the reform of the health insurance program, the administration was able to include a major change in the student loan program. By eliminating fees paid to private banks that have acted as intermediaries in providing loans to college students, the government will be able to save billions of dollars, expand Pell grants, and at the same time, "make it easier for students to repay outstanding loans after graduating."[8]

In addition, Pell grants will be increased during the next several years. The White House predicted that the change will result in "820,000 more grants by 2020." President Obama commented that these changes were a victory over an "army of lobbyists." He noted that Sallie Mae, which was the largest firm engaged in the student loan program, had "spent $3 million on lobbying to stop the changes." The downside of the change is the loss of jobs in the banking industry. Senator Lamar Alexander predicted that the changes in the lending process "would cost 31,000 private-sector jobs."[9]

Even with these reforms, the problem of helping students and their families meet the ever-increasing cost of college remains a major issue. A *New York Times* article in October of 2009 included the fact that because of "state budget cuts, four-year public colleges raised tuition and fees by an average of 6.5 percent" during the 2008–2009 college year. Private colleges raised their total costs at the rate of 4.4 percent. Currently, the average cost of attending a four-year public college is $15,213. Private colleges on average are charging $35,636 per year.[10]

In some states, the cost of attending a public college is growing in large part because these institutions are receiving less state assistance. For example, in California in 2009, the increase in undergraduate fees, which is "the equivalent of tuition," rose by 32 percent. This will make the cost of attending the University of California to be "about three times as much as it was a decade ago." The dramatic increases caused Tamar Lewin to write in the *New York Times* that a state college in California was "beginning to look more like a private institution."[11]

Historically, it has been true that state colleges have been available to students from families who were unable or unwilling to pay the higher tuition at private colleges. Unless enough financial aid from the states can be made available to maintain the cost gap, public colleges will continue to have problems. While higher education in general is a major priority of the Obama administration, increased attention to one component of the higher education system is receiving much of the attention.

Because of the desire to improve K–12 education, the administration is also seeking ways to improve the way we educate our teachers. Barack Obama's campaign literature as a presidential candidate recognized the need to improve the preparation of teachers. Among the programs called for in a public document titled "Barack Obama's Plan for Lifetime Success through Education" are the following:

- The creation of "substantial, sustained Teacher Service Scholarships that completely cover training costs in high-quality teacher preparation or alternative certification programs at the undergraduate or graduate level for those who are willing to teach in a high-need field or location for at least four years.
- Professional accreditation of all programs preparing teachers, with a focus on evidence regarding how well teachers are prepared. In order to help identify the most successful programs, colleges of education and alternative licensure programs will track their graduates' entry and retention in teaching and their contributions to growth in student learning. Challenge grants will encourage the adoption of successful practices across the entire enterprise of teacher preparation.
- The development of a high-quality, nationally available teacher performance assessment that measures actual teaching skill in content areas.
- The establishment of professional development schools that will enable teachers to learn from practitioners in the field. Like teaching hospitals in medicine, professional development schools partner universities with school sites that exhibit state-of-the-art practice and train new teachers in the classrooms of expert teachers while they are completing course work.
- Legislation to create teaching residency programs to prepare teachers to work in high-need districts.[12]

The impetus for improving what is happening in the field of teacher education has been encouraged as a result of a series of public criticisms of current programs. Typical of these attacks was a National Public Radio report by Claudio Sanchez. In the program, former president of Columbia University Teachers College Arthur Levine was quoted as saying, "Education schools have, in many cases, become irrelevant and often of low quality." Leila Christenbury, a professor at Virginia Commonwealth University, was also quoted as saying, "Some education professors are clueless about kids and just about everything else that happens in classrooms these days."[13]

The story went on to suggest that "the curriculum at schools of education has little to do with practice. . . . There's a gap that's a mile wide. Senior professors don't participate in schools. There are universities around this country that place their students for student teaching in failing schools with failing teachers. That's a major problem."[14]

Another issue mentioned in the same broadcast was the fact that of the 1,300 schools of education, only about half are nationally accredited. Even in accredited programs, it was suggested that there is not a great deal of quality research being produced.[15] Within the ranks of teacher education programs, there is also criticism of how we are training teachers. Katherine Merseth, director of teacher education at the Harvard Graduate School of Education, publicly charged that only about a hundred of the colleges of education are doing a competent job, and it is her opinion that "the others could be shut down tomorrow."[16]

Perhaps the main criticism of teacher preparation programs has become the failure to adequately prepare teachers who can work successfully in urban schools. Scott Gaiber has written that urban teachers must be trained "to mediate the myriad ways that poverty, culture, and language affect low-income children's development and possess the instructional tools to drastically improve student academic performance."[17]

He goes on to claim that we "train our teachers in a generic manner without taking into account geographic or demographic differences in teaching environments." In making the case for special efforts to train teachers to work in the city, Gaiber notes the obstacles that students in the city face. These include "poverty, less access to quality health care, subpar living conditions, higher rates of single-parent families, higher rates of violence in their communities, and lower levels of parent income." He argues that these factors cause urban students to lag behind their fellow students who live in the suburbs or in rural areas.[18]

Criticisms such as those noted above have led the National Council for Accreditation of Teacher Education (NCATE) to begin to revise its accreditation programs. What is being developed is a plan that requires teacher education programs that are seeking NCATE accreditation to change their approach. James Cibulka, president of NCATE, has commented that "in the past, accreditation wrapped clinical experience around course work." He suggested that the approach being developed will reverse "the priority, encouraging institutions to place teacher candidates in year-long training programs and wrap course work around clinical practice."[19]

The idea is to have teacher education students work for an extended period in schools in the same way that medical residents are required to work in hospitals. Course work required for teaching would center on real experiences, especially in high-need schools. This would be consistent with the objectives of the Obama administration, as it will "close the gap between theory and practice, and ensure that teacher candidates are able to help diverse students be successful."[20]

The goals of the new initiatives in the accreditation of teacher education programs go beyond just improving the way our nation educates its future teachers. The more far-reaching hope is to make "teaching a more respected profession." This, too, would be an important aspect of the agenda of the Obama administration. In October of 2009, Secretary Duncan told an audience at Columbia University Teachers College that "teaching should be one of our most revered professions, and teacher preparation programs should be among a university's most important responsibilities."[21]

Overall, there seems to be a growing sense that in order to improve the profession we must "bridge 'the yawning chasm of practice and theory between the universities and the schools.' . . . Our programs must become more like 'teaching hospitals.'" According to James Cibulka, "the ivory tower and the little red school house must learn to work together."[22]

Attempting to improve teacher education programs will not be easy. Since their inception in many colleges and universities, they have not been respected or given adequate financial support. As Secretary Duncan said in his speech at Columbia, these programs "have frequently been treated like the Rodney Dangerfield of higher education. Historically, education schools were the institutions that got no respect from the Oval Office to the Provost's Office, from university presidents to Secretaries of Education."[23]

Noting that this has been going on for a long time, the secretary quoted a Harvard president in the 1930s, describing Harvard Graduate School of Education as a "kitten that ought to be drowned." He also referred to Arthur Powell's book *The Uncertain Profession*, in which the author claimed that "none of the social sciences spawned by the American university at the end of the nineteenth century has had a more volatile and troublesome history than the field of education."[24]

Additional critics of teacher education mentioned by Secretary Duncan include former Harvard president James Bryant Conan, who reported that "many students believe their required courses at the ed school were 'Mickey Mouse' courses." Finally, Duncan turned to the classic book *Teacher in America*, by Jacques Barzun, which contains the charge that "teacher training is based on a strong anti-intellectual bias enhanced by a total lack of imagination."[25]

While the secretary blamed higher education for the quality of our education schools, he noted that the states, as well as the federal government, were "also culpable for the persistence of weak preparation programs." He faulted the fact that states produced low-quality certification exams and did little to encourage school district mentoring programs for new teachers.[26]

Another issue related to the effort to transform teacher education is the support of the Obama administration for alternate route programs. For some time, states have developed plans allowing candidates with bachelor's degrees in an academic area to enter such programs. Sometimes referred to as "shortcut" programs to teacher certification, a person with an appropriate academic background can be certified to teach in less than a year. As early as 2002, forty-five states had initiated alternative teacher education programs.[27]

This trend has been supported by the federal government, which has allotted millions of dollars to assist colleges to create this opportunity for potential teachers. In some cases, the student's tuition is paid for by a school district, and upon completion of as little as one summer of academic work, a student can assume a teaching job. In certain urban areas, a job is guaranteed to a person accepted into the program.[28]

Currently, the trend for expanding alternate route programs has become much stronger. For over a century, education schools have had "a virtual monopoly on the teaching profession." In New York State, the possibility of allowing alternative organizations to create their own master's degree programs will put them in direct competition with college teacher education programs. For Arthur Levine, a past president of Teachers College of Columbia University, "Education schools are on the verge of losing their franchise." For instance, in Rhode Island and Louisiana, alternative programs are already allowed to grant teacher certification to their own graduates.[29]

Such programs have generated considerable criticism from some teacher educators. A study in 2007 pointed to the following problems:

• Entry standards are abysmally low. Two-thirds of the programs surveyed accept half or more of their teacher applicants; one-quarter accept virtually everyone who applies.
• Rather than providing streamlined and effective course work, about a third of the programs require at least thirty hours of education school courses—the same amount needed for a master's degree.
• Most disturbing, nearly 70 percent of alternative programs studied in the report are run by education schools themselves. Education schools have kept their market monopoly by moving into the alternative certification business.[30]

Linda Darling-Hammond, an education adviser to the president during his campaign, is a critic of alternate route programs. For her, the method being proposed by NCATE, which models itself after the way doctors are prepared, is the appropriate method for training teachers. She points out that we are currently subsidizing medical education programs and teaching hospitals and that we should do the same for preparing teachers. In addition, she has recommended "scholarships for well-qualified candidates, along with 'recruitment incentives' to 'attract and retain expert, experienced teachers in high-needs schools.'"[31]

The growing popularity of alternative route programs is likely to continue. This will be especially true in the areas of math, science, and technology. As pointed out by C. Emily Feistritzer in *Education Week*, "About one-third of new teachers hired in this country" are graduates of the six hundred alternative route programs, which are available in "nearly every state." It is likely that many states will apply for and receive Race to the Top money to fund such programs.[32]

Other suggestions for improving teacher education programs have come from a report released by Strategic Management of Human Capital. Among the well-known members of this task force were Michelle A. Rhee, chancellor of the District of Columbia schools, and Joel I. Klein, chancellor of the New York City schools. One of their recommendations included "raising the bar for who can enter undergraduate-level teacher education programs— perhaps by requiring a minimum score on the SAT or the ACT." They also recommended a more "rigorous content test before prospective teachers can earn an initial teaching license."[33]

While the criticisms of teacher training programs have been frequent, occasionally they have been defended by those who feel that our problems in education should not be laid primarily at the feet of our education programs. Professor of Education Pedro A. Noguera takes issue with Secretary Duncan's comment that schools of education are "mediocre" and that they are failing to produce teachers who are prepared to teach in the public schools. Noguera believes that "it makes no more sense to blame schools of education for the failings of public schools than it does to blame business schools for the collapse of our country's financial sector."[34]

While admitting that "many schools of education don't recruit the best students into the profession," he believes that "the best students are attracted to more-lucrative careers." He goes on to talk about several ways to improve what we are doing in our teacher preparation programs. Among his suggestions are these:

• Provide financial incentives for schools of education to establish lab schools in high-need areas, so that new and inexperienced teachers can receive training in best practices in educational settings that approximate the conditions in the schools where they will actually work.

- Offer debt relief beyond the federal TEACH grant program to math and science majors who pursue teaching careers, on the condition that they stay in the profession for more than five years (unlike Teach for America fellows, who typically remain no more than two or three years).
- Create encouragement for leading universities to do more than leave to their schools of education the problem of training teachers. We could provide incentives to scholars from the arts, humanities, and sciences to work with teachers to develop innovative curricula.
- Provide incentives like work-study programs to enlist undergraduates to work in high-need schools as tutors and mentors.

He ends his article by suggesting that "Secretary Duncan would be more likely to move the nation's education agenda forward if he did less scolding and more encouraging."[35]

Others writing about the future of teacher education suggest that there might be something to learn by studying the transformation of college programs in business education. One author highlights the academic rigor that was introduced into the best MBA programs. A similar demanding curriculum could not only improve what students are learning but also increase the status of education programs within the academic community.[36]

In January of 2010, the president himself expressed his own feelings about teacher training. He said that "teacher quality is the most important single factor that influences whether students succeed or fail." He was referring primarily to the so-called STEM fields of science, technology, engineering, and math. He pointed to the $250 million in public and private investments in the Educate to Innovate campaign, which is designed to help train more than 100,000 teachers during the next five years. The importance of this objective can be seen in his comment, "Make no mistake: our future is on the line. . . . The nation that out-educates us today is going to out-compete us tomorrow."[37]

In his 2010 State of the Union address, President Obama talked about the need to "revitalize our community colleges" and to make all colleges and universities more affordable, because "in the United States of America, no one should go broke because they choose to go to college."[38] It is not surprising that the president should reiterate his commitment to higher education, as he has been consistent in supporting additional federal financing and change, especially in the preparation of teachers.

Whether or not it will be possible to further increase the federal role in higher education will depend on the pace of economic recovery and future political developments. Even though it is not totally within his control, given his past comments and record, we can expect Barack Obama to maintain higher education as a major priority for his administration. While assistance to colleges has long been a cause championed by the president, his support of several other education initiatives has emerged since taking office. One of these issues is the effort to give to mayors of cities additional power to manage their school districts.

NOTES

1. Arlene Cherwin, "Obama and Higher Education: Promises and Problems," *University World News*, 9 November 2008, www.universityworldnews.com/article .php?story=20081106155912850 (accessed 20 January 2010).

2. "The Administration's Higher Education Agenda," *Congressweb.com*, www .congressweb.com/aascu/obama_higher_ed.htm (accessed 28 September 2009).

3. Michele McNeil and Alyson Klein, "President's Education Aims Aired," *Education Digest*, May 2009, 16.

4. "Obama Remarks on Higher Education," *Washington Post*, 24 April 2009, www.washingtonpost.com/wp-dyn/content/article/2009/04/24/ar2009042402380 .html (accessed 20 January 2010).

5. Nick Anderson, "Obama Seeks to Expand Student Loan Program," *Washington Post*, 25 January 2010, www.washingtonpost.com/wp-dyn/content/article/ 2010/01/25/ar2010012501813.html (accessed 26 January 2010).

6. Catherine Gewertz, "Help with Aid Form Found to Boost College-Going," *Education Week*, 23 September 2009, www.edweek.org/ew/articles/2009/09/23/05fafsa .h29.html (accessed 25 September 2009).

7. Nick Anderson, "Duncan Promotes Simpler College Financial Aid Application," *Washington Post*, 6 January 2010, www.washingtonpost.com/wp-dyn/content/ article/2010/01/05/ar2010010501174.html (accessed 6 January 2010).

8. Peter Baker and David M. Herszenhorn, "Obama Signs Overhaul of Student Loan Program," *New York Times*, 30 March 2010, www.nytimes.com/2010/03/31/us/ politics/31obama.html?ref=education (accessed 6 April 2010).

9. Ibid.

10. Tamar Lewin, "College Costs Keep Rising, Report Says," *New York Times*, 20 October 2009, www.nytimes.com/2009/10/21/education/21costs.html? _r=1&ref=education (accessed 27 October 2009).

11. Tamar Lewin, "A Crown Jewel of Education Struggles with Cuts," *New York Times*, 19 November 2009, www.nytimes.com/2009/11/20/education/20/ education/20berkley.html?_r=1&ref=education (accessed 23 November 2009).

12. "Barack Obama's Plan for Lifetime Success through Education," *Obama for America*, 6–7.

13. Claudio Sanchez, "What Should Go into a Teaching Degree?" *National Public Radio*, 30 September 2009, www.npr.org/templates/story/story.php?storyid=11349924 (accessed 2 October 2009).

14. Ibid.

15. Ibid.

16. The Editors, "Do Teachers Need Education Degrees?" *New York Times*, 16 August 2009, roomfordebate.blogs.nytimes.com/2009/08/16/education-degrees-and -teachers-pay/ (accessed 17 August 2009).

17. Scott Gaiber, "Closing the Teacher Preparation Gap," *PolicyMatters*, 2009, www.policymatters.net, 14–15.

18. Ibid.

19. "A New Approach to Teacher Education," *American Teacher*, September 2009, 7.

20. Ibid.

21. Jennifer Epstein, "Making Teaching a Profession," *Inside Higher Ed*, 5 January 2010, www.insidehighered.com/layout/set/print/news/2010/01/05/teachers (accessed 8 January 2010).

22. Ibid.

23. "Teacher Preparation: Reforming the Uncertain Profession—Remarks of Secretary Arne Duncan at Teachers College, Columbia University," *Ed.gov*, 22 October 2009, www.edgov/news/speeches/2009/10/10222009.html (accessed 4 November 2009).

24. Ibid.

25. Ibid.

26. Ibid.

27. William Hayes, *No Child Left Behind: Past, Present, and Future* (Lanham, Md.: Rowman & Littlefield Education, 2008), 85.

28. Ibid.

29. Lisa W. Foderaro, "Alternate Path for Teachers Gains Ground," *New York Times*, 18 April 2010, www.nytimes.com/2010/04/19/education/19regents.html ?ref=education (accessed 20 April 2010).

30. Kate Walsh, "Alternative Certification Isn't Alternative," Thomas B. Fordham Institute, 18 September 2007, www.edexcellence.net/institute/publication/publication .cfm?id=375 (accessed 21 September 2007).

31. Linda Darling-Hammond, "A Marshall Plan for Teaching," *Education Week*, 9 January 2007, www.guilfordeducationalliance.org/documents/EdWeekMarshallPlan1 -10-07.pdf (accessed 17 October 2007).

32. C. Emily Feistritzer, "How Teacher Preparation Has Changed and Why It May Need to Change More," *Education Week*, 20 November 2009, www.edweek.org/ew/ articles/2009/11/18/12feistritzer.h29.html (accessed 20 November 2009).

33. Lesli A. Maxwell, "National Panel Urges Upgrades to Teacher Workforce," *Education Week*, 4 November 2009, www.edweek.org/ew/articles/2009/11/04/11smhc _ep.h29.html (accessed 4 November 2009).

34. Pedro A. Noguera, "The New War against Ed Schools," *Education Week*, 16 November 2009, www.edweek.org/ew/articles/2009/11/18/12noguera.h29.html (accessed 20 November 2009).

35. Ibid.

36. Robert Maranto, Gary Ritter, and Arthur E. Levine, "Five Lessons from Business Schools," *Education Week*, 5 January 2010, www.edweek.org/ew/articles/2010/01/06/16maranto_ep.h29.html (accessed 6 January 2010).

37. Charles Dharapak, "Obama Announces Teacher Training Initiative," *USA Today*, 6 January 2010, www.usatoday.com/news/education/2010-01-06-obama -education_n.htm (accessed 20 January 2010).

38. "Remarks by the President in State of the Union Address," *whitehouse.gov*, 27 January 2010, www.whitehouse.gov/the-press-office/remarks-president-state-union -address (accessed 2 February 2010).

12

Mayoral Control of Schools in Urban Districts

Secretary of Education Duncan has made it absolutely clear that he favors strong mayoral control over urban schools. The president himself has thus far said little about this issue. Still, reporters who have heard him speak have concluded that he is, indeed, in favor of this initiative. On March 11, 2009, Philissa Cramer noted that the editorial board of the *New York Post* interpreted a speech made in New York City by the president as "a ringing endorsement of . . . mayoral control."[1] A journalist covering a speech by Obama in Milwaukee, in November of 2009, wrote that "Obama made it clear that he believes in mayoral control of urban school districts."[2]

While it is difficult to find conclusive evidence of the president's personal feelings on this issue, this is certainly not true for Secretary Duncan. *New Republic* reported in the April 2009 issue that Secretary Duncan "advocated for mayoral control of big-city school systems, which places the vast majority of power over educational policy and logistics in mayors' offices. Currently, seven cities have mayoral control, including Chicago, Duncan's old stomping ground." Secretary Duncan is quoted as saying that he "will have failed" if more urban districts are not being controlled by mayors. He made clear that he's "willing to go personally from district to district pushing the cause."[3]

Speaking in Madison, Wisconsin, in November of 2009, the secretary was quoted as saying, "A place like Milwaukee has flatlined. . . . It's not making the progress it needs to make." To move forward, Duncan endorsed the idea of mayoral control, which was being considered in the city at the time of his visit.[4] Even though the administration supports the transfer of power to mayors, it is not clear that the Democratic Party shares this enthusiasm. Alan J.

Borsuk said in an article in the *Milwaukee Journal Sentinel* that in Wisconsin at least, there are Democrats on both sides of the issue.[5] The party is split in New York State as well. During the debate over whether Mayor Bloomberg's control of New York City schools should be extended, a number of state senators charged that the mayor's "control is not only dangerously authoritative, but also misleading, as some believe that his reported school improvements are inaccurate." They accused Bloomberg "of massaging statistics and focusing on teaching to standardized tests."[6]

Not only do Obama and Duncan have to contend with members of their own party who have negative feelings about the issue, but they are also in danger of angering many teachers who are unenthusiastic about this proposed change of power. For example, in Rochester, New York, the president of the local teachers union, Adam Urbanski, has made it clear that his local union would oppose giving control of that city's schools to Mayor Robert Duffy.[7]

On the other hand, in a joint appearance with Secretary Duncan, American Federation of Teachers president Randi Weingarten defended Mayor Bloomberg's work in New York City. She is quoted as saying, "Mayoral control with some checks and balances will help drive school improvement."[8] The division in union sentiment is shown by the fact that while Weingarten is the president of the American Federation of Teachers, Adam Urbanski is a vice president of the same organization.

Despite the lack of endorsement of many of his supporters, it is extremely unlikely that President Obama would be allowing his secretary of education to travel around the country touting a policy he did not believe in. This is especially true because the change to mayoral control would fundamentally alter the governance structure of our public schools. Local school boards have been in existence since early in our colonial period. In Massachusetts in 1647, a law was passed giving to the local communities the responsibility to establish schools. This law created the first school boards in what was to become the United States.[9]

The practice of electing community citizens to manage our schools spread to every state during the eighteenth and nineteenth centuries. The rationale for local control is discussed in an article written by David Tyack in 1999.

Under . . . local control, school trustees constituted the most numerous class of public officials in the world; in some states, there were as many as 45,000 local school trustees, often outnumbering teachers. Decentralized governance addressed public distrust of government by putting the school and its trustees everywhere under the eye and thumb of the citizens. This provided democracy in education, meaning self-rule by elected representatives of the people. Communities were able to retain collective decisions about schooling—who would teach, how much schools would cost, and what kind of instruction to offer. If district voters disagreed with school trustees, they could elect others.[10]

During the so-called progressive period at the beginning of the twentieth century, there was a movement to "expunge politics from schooling." The idea was to leave the day-to-day management of schools in the hands of highly trained educational administrators and to "insulate them from political abuses." In doing so, communities were assured that mayors would have little or no control over the schools in their cities. The effort to eliminate political influence from school governance caused historian Charles Beard to observe that "cities change from one [approach] to the other in the hope—usually vain—of taking the school affairs out of the spoils system."[11]

Realizing that the push for mayoral control will undoubtedly be controversial, it is important to attempt to identify the advantages and disadvantages of such a system. Those supporting the change would point to the following arguments:

- What we are doing in most of our city schools is not working.
- We are having an unacceptable level of turnover among urban school superintendents. In a speech in Baltimore in 2009, Secretary Duncan alluded to the fact that in the past ten years the city of Baltimore had had seven superintendents. He raised the question "What business would run this way?"[12]
- Giving mayors additional power in education would create a "clear line of accountability to one person" rather than a large bureaucracy.[13]
- The transfer of power has worked in cities such as Boston, Chicago, and New York, where there have been "improved test scores." It also has been noted that in these cities, superintendents appointed by the mayor have remained in the district longer and teacher strikes have been avoided.[14]
- It must be remembered that abolishing a local school board does not take away the public's right to elect those who will manage our schools. Both the mayor and the members of the city council are officials elected by the entire community.[15]
- It should be noted also that superintendents may continue to play an important leadership role in their school districts, even when they report directly to the mayor. A profile in *District Administration* highlights the contributions of Harrisburg, Pennsylvania, Superintendent Gerald Kohn. In 2001, this school district was ranked last among the state's 501 school districts. By 2005, there was a 71 percent increase in the high school graduation rate, and seven of the twelve elementary schools had made "adequate yearly progress" under the provisions of the No Child Left

Behind Act.[16] Even with these accomplishments, the newly elected mayor of Harrisburg, Linda Thompson, has vowed to lobby the state legislature to reinstate an elected school board for the city.[17] Here, as in other cities, even when mayoral control appears to be successful, there will be those who oppose the system.

The arguments of those who are critical of the initiative could be summarized as follows:

- Michael Resnick, an official of the National School Boards Association, has argued that local school boards "are the backbone of community representatives in schools. . . . Education is too important to fall into the already lengthy list of functions mayors are managing."[18]
- Elected boards of education almost always include a significant number of parents. These are people who have personal interest in the schools. Appointed school boards or even elected city councils might lack adequate parental input.[19]
- Like superintendents, mayors also change, and while one might do a great job with schools, the next mayor could be a disaster.[20]
- Well-known educator Gerald Bracey begins his essay on the subject by questioning Secretary Duncan's record as a chief school officer appointed by the mayor of Chicago. He points out that "in 2003, 4 percent of Chicago's black eighth-graders were proficient or better in math and by 2007, the figure had risen to 6 percent." He also attacked the Panel for Educational Policy appointed by Mayor Bloomberg in New York City. He referred to a story in the *New York Times* that described the panelists as "an investment banker, a lingerie store owner, and an expert on electromagnetics" and suggested that the group "rarely engage in discussions with those who rise to address them. They do not debate the educational issues of the day, but spend most sessions applauding packaged presentations by staff. Some have barely uttered a public word during their tenures."[21]
- Diane Ravitch has also publicly opposed a shift of educational responsibilities to city mayors. She wrote: "Mayoral control is no solution to poor academic performance. It may or may not lead to better, more efficient provision of services. . . . Anyone who looks at mayoral control of urban schools as a panacea will be disappointed." Using the federally administered tests (NAEP) that are considered "the gold standard of the testing industry," she points out the lack of evidence supporting mayoral control. On tests given in eleven cities since 2003, "the highest performing districts were Charlotte, North Carolina, and Austin, Texas, neither

of which is controlled by their mayor. The lowest performing districts were Washington, D.C., Chicago, Illinois, and Cleveland, Ohio. The public schools in Chicago and Cleveland have been controlled by their mayor for more than a decade."[22]

• In Flint, Michigan, where a debate is raging over the issue, Kelly E. Flynn has argued that "mayoral control is about pleasing the business community and privatizing education." It takes power "out of the hands of the community" and places it in the hands of a mayor and "a board appointed by the mayor, rather than the democratic representation of an elected school board." She believes that mayors should worry about community centers and keeping kids off the street. For Flynn, mayoral control "seems at odds with President Obama's dedication to public discourse, transparency, and grass-roots government."[23]

The strong feelings of opposition to mayoral control were evident in July of 2009 during the fight to renew Mayor Bloomberg's powers in New York City. Speakers at a demonstration opposing the continuation of the mayor's powers told a crowd that democracy had to be returned to the school system and to classrooms and that "parents and the community" should be given "a larger role in their children's public education."[24]

In almost every community where the idea of mayoral control of the schools has been introduced, there has been a heated and emotional debate both in public meetings and in the media. As with so many controversial issues, definitive research is unavailable, even though both sides of the issue can point to examples that they feel support their position.

A report by the Center for the Study of Social Policy in 2005 concluded that "there is no clear evidence that mayoral takeovers improve student achievement or fiscal efficiency." Another authority, Frederick M. Hess, has written, "While some researchers have demonstrated some evidence that mayoral control may be linked to improved performance, the systematic evidence is only modestly illuminating. Caution is recommended when making strong claims" about its effectiveness.[25]

Another major research study at Brown University, published in 2007, addressed the issue by considering "student outcomes and management improvement" using a "mixed-methods approach, including case studies and statistical analysis using a multiyear database on a purposeful sample of 100 urban districts." Several of the conclusions reached in the study follow:

• Mayoral-appointed school boards have shown measurable accomplishment, including significant academic improvement and more efficient financial and administrative management.

- Mayoral control brings a strong emphasis on academic accountability, which seems consistent with the public expectation in the context of the No Child Left Behind law.
- Although districts vary in reform effectiveness, mayoral-appointed boards seem to be able to establish clear and attainable strategic goals.
- Mayors seem to be willing to put financial and political resources into leveling up failing schools.
- Mayoral leadership is likely to benefit from broader community engagement.
- As mayoral control settles in across the nation, the long-term effects of the reform can begin to be evaluated. With comparable data for a longer (10-plus years) period, we can answer questions about sustainability and possible cyclical effects.[26]

In regard to the final point made in the report noted above, all of the authorities agree that there is a need for long-term research to determine if the change in management responsibilities for schools will have a lasting impact. In addition, it is important to note that currently it is Secretary Duncan, rather than the president, who is leading the offensive for mayoral control.

Barack Obama, at some point, will have to determine whether he is willing to risk another conflict with some of his supporters in the educational establishment. Along with perhaps upsetting some teachers, administrators, and school board members, he can also expect to hear from unhappy members of his political party. As always, like every president, he will have to pick his political battles.

The president has already spoken frequently about another issue that is also undoubtedly controversial. In this case, he is advocating a course of action that will affect the lives of every student, as well as their family members. The president would very much like to increase the time that students spend in the classroom. This can mean either longer school days or an extension of the school calendar. This proposal is the subject of our next chapter.

NOTES

1. Philissa Cramer, "Gotham Schools—Daily Reporting on NYC Public Schools," *Gothamschools.org*, 11 March 2009, gothamschools.org/2009/03/11/post-obamas -speech-shows-hes-a-mayoral-control-fan/ (accessed 12 February 2010).

2. "Obama's Upcoming Visit Intensifies Mayoral Takeover Debate," *wisn.com*, 2 November 2009, www.wisn.com/education/21503072/detail.html (accessed 11 February 2010).

3. Seyward Darby, "Duncan Wades into the School Control Debate," *New Republic*, 1 April 2009, www.tnr.com/blog/the-plank/duncan-wades-the-school-control-debate (accessed 10 February 2010).

4. Scott Bauer, "Obama's Visit in Midst of Education Debate," *Dailyreporter. com*, 3 November 2009, dailyreporter.com/blog/2009/11/03/obama-visits-state-in-midst-of-education-debate-413-pm-11309/ (accessed 11 February 2010).

5. Alan J. Borsuk, "Democrats Sit on Both Sides of Debates on Mayoral Control, Performance Pay," *Milwaukee Journal Sentinel*, 12 September 2009, www.jsonline.com/news/education/59142092.html (accessed 18 September 2009).

6. Grace Chen, "Are City Mayors Taking Control over Public Schools?" *Public School Review*, 30 July 2009, www.publicschoolreview.com/articles/130 (accessed 11 February 2010).

7. Dakarai Aarons, "Rochester, N.Y., Mayor Wants Control of Schools," *Education Week*, 29 December 2009, blogs.edweek.org/edweek/District_Dossier/2009/12/rochester_ny_mayor_wants_school.html (accessed 4 January 2010).

8. "Weingarten, Mulgrew on Panels at National Action Network Conference," *United Federation of Teachers*, 23 April 2009, www.uft.org/news/teacher/top/discuss_mayoral_control/ (accessed 11 February 2010).

9. William Drake, *The American School in Transition* (New York: Prentice Hall, 1955), 71.

10. David Tyack, "Democracy in Education—Who Needs It?" *Education Week*, 17 November 1999, www.edweek.org/ew/ewstory.cfm?slug=12TYACK.h19&keywords=David%20tyack (accessed 24 February 2010).

11. Charles Beard, *American City Government: A Survey of New Tendencies* (New York: Arno, 1970), 314.

12. Sara Neufeld, "Duncan Supports Mayoral Control of Schools . . . in Baltimore?" *Baltimore Sun*, 1 April 2009, weblogs.baltimoresun.com/news/education/blog/2009/04/baltimore_schools_arne_duncan.html (accessed 11 February 2010).

13. Michele McNeil, "Arne and Co. Tackle Mayoral Control," *Education Week*, 6 July 2009, blogs.edweek.org/edweek/campaign-k-12/2009/07/arne_and_co_tackle_mayoral_con.html (accessed 11 February 2010).

14. Martha T. Moore, "More Mayors Move to Take over Schools, *USA Today*, 22 March 2007, www.usatoday.com/news/education/2007-03-20-covers-mayors-schools_n.htm (accessed 3 February 2010).

15. Mary Anna Towler, "Let the Mayor Run the Schools," *City*, 30 December 2009, 2–3.

16. Stephanie Johns, "Measuring Success in Harrisburg," *District Administration*, October 2009, 39.

17. Ron Schachter, "Tell It to the Mayor," *District Administration*, August 2009, 24.

18. Libby Quaid, "School Chief: Mayors Need Control of Urban Schools," *Brown University*, 5 February 2010, www.brown.edu/departments/education/news/20090406_kwong_ap_article.php (accessed 11 February 2010).

19. John Hechinger and Suzanne Sataline, "For More Mayors, School Takeovers Are a No-Brainer," *Wall Street Journal*, 12 March 2009, online.wsj.com/article/sb123682041297603203.html (accessed 11 February 2010).

20. Ibid.

21. Gerald Bracey, "Mayoral Control of Schools: The New Tyranny," *Huffington Post*, 21 July 2009, www.huffingtonpost.com/gerald-bracey/mayoral-control-of-school_b _240487.html (accessed 11 February 2010).

22. Diane Ravitch, "The Myth of Mayoral Control of Schools," *Huffington Post*, 11 February 2009, www.huffingtonpost.com/diane-ravitch/the-myth-of-mayoral -contr_b_191072.html (accessed 11 February 2010).

23. Kelly E. Flynn, "Mayoral Control of Schools Is at Odds with Grass-Roots Government," *mlive.com*, 19 April 2009, www.mlive.com/opinion/flint/index .ssf/2009/04/post_20.html (accessed 11 February 2010).

24. Nayaba Arinde and Maryam Abdul-Aleem, "Activists Call Mayoral School Control 'Illegal,'" *New York Amsterdam News*, 9 July 2009.

25. Frederick M. Hess, "Assessing the Case for Mayoral Control of Urban Schools," *AEI Outlook Series*, August 2008, www.aei.org/outlook/28511 (accessed 11 February 2010).

26. Kenneth K. Wong, "Mayoral Leadership Matters: Lessons Learned from Mayoral Control of Large Urban School Systems," *Peabody Journal of Education*, 2007, 765–66.

13

More Time in School

It would seem to be common sense that if students spent more time in class-rooms with their teachers, they would learn more and have better test results. Since taking office, "both President Obama and Education Secretary Arne Duncan have called the traditional school day and school year outdated and inadequate for the demands of the 21st century life." They have also commented on the fact that "students in countries that routinely outscore the United States on international tests go to school for as many as 230 days each year, 50 more than kids typically attend here." During a speech to a group of students in Denver, Duncan said to his audience, "Go ahead and boo me. . . . I think schools should be open six, seven days a week, eleven, twelve months a year."[1]

The current school calendar used by most school districts in the United States emerged when the country was still primarily made up of farm families. Students in these classrooms, which were often in one-room schools, were needed to work on their family farms during the summer months and often in the spring. Because the vast majority of Americans were Christians, time was also taken off for celebrating both Christmas and Easter. Even as families moved into the cities and later to the suburbs, the school calendar settled at its present 180 days.

In recent years, a number of these days have been allowed to be used for testing purposes, teacher in-service days, and parent conferences. The result has been that schools are often likely to have no more than 170 days for actual instruction. In addition, it is also true that the school day in the United States is shorter than in many other countries. In a significant number of suburbs and rural areas, it is not unusual for students to spend more than an hour a day on a school bus. Elementary school administrators and parents are often concerned about when to begin their school day because they don't wish to have their students walking to school or waiting for the bus too early in the morning.

At the high school level, most public schools have an active extracurricular schedule in the late afternoons. This includes not only athletic events but also club meetings and musical activities. Teachers and many parents prefer that these activities take place after school rather than in the evening. As far as starting schools earlier in the morning, it is thought that many adolescents do not perform well in early morning classes.

Spending more time in school is also considered a problem for some school employees. While many school administrators work a twelve-month calendar and might be less opposed to adding school days, they might also admit that during school vacations, their schedules are much less stressful. Teachers and school staff often have stronger feelings about the issue. If extra time in class results in an increase in salaries, many teachers and staff members might welcome an extended day or calendar. On the other hand, there are those who greatly appreciate the long vacations for the additional time they can spend with their families. This dichotomy of views makes it difficult for teachers unions to develop a position on this issue.

In any case, proponents of change in the daily schedule or the school year must accept the reality that it will add expenses to the school budget. Along with additional salaries and fringe benefits, the district will undoubtedly see an increase in student transportation costs. Heating and electric bills are also likely to be affected. Besides the faculty, there would be additional expenses to pay for some nonteaching personnel. Even with these concerns, the idea of extending the time students spend in class continues to be a topic of discussion in many areas.

In February of 2007, the *Dallas News* carried an Associated Press story headlined "Length of School Day under Review across Nation." The state of Massachusetts was used as one example of an area "putting in place the longer-day model." Legislators were also engaged in debates about the issue in Minnesota, New Mexico, New York, and Washington, D.C. Charter schools, since their inception, have often utilized extended classroom time and even longer calendars.[2]

An example is the Knowledge Is Power Program (KIPP), which manages charter schools in locations throughout the nation. In these schools, which usually serve "low-income middle-school students," there is some evidence of higher test scores. Their programs are in session from 7:30 a.m. to 5:00 p.m. during the week and for a few hours every other Saturday. In addition, the students attend school for several weeks in the summer.[3]

In 2007, to carry out this schedule, these charter schools were spending an additional $1,200 per student to achieve 50 percent more instructional time for their students. At that time, the state of Massachusetts had begun its own experimental program for the public schools, which was costing an additional $1,300 for every student on the extended schedule. There it was noted that senior teachers were making as much as $20,000 more a year for taking on additional teaching responsibilities. When Massachusetts introduced this schedule for some of its schools, the National Education Association took no official position either in support of or in opposition to the idea.[4]

While the unions have been quiet, President Obama, like his secretary of education, has publicly supported a longer school year. During his third month in office, the *Seattle Times* reported that the president had publicly taken the position that American students "should go to school longer—either stay later in the day or into the summer—if they're going to have any chance of competing for jobs and paychecks against foreign kids."[5]

He went on to say, "We can no longer afford an academic calendar designed when America was a nation of farmers who needed their children at home plowing the land at the end of the day. . . . That calendar may have once made sense, but today, it puts us at a competitive disadvantage. Our children spend over a month less in school than children in South Korea. That is no way to prepare them for a 21st century economy." Like Secretary Duncan, the president has acknowledged publicly that even with his own daughters, longer school days and school years are not "wildly popular ideas."[6]

In the same speech, President Obama again pointed to test scores as a reason for increasing the time students spend in school. His comments included the statement, "Despite resources that are unmatched anywhere in the world, we have let our grades slip, our schools crumble, our teacher quality fall short and other nations to outpace us." He gave the example that "in eighth-grade math, we've fallen to ninth place. Singapore's middle-schoolers outperform ours 3-to-1. Just a third of our 13 and 14-year-olds can read as well as they should."[7]

Secretary Duncan has taken up the cause by giving examples of schools that have had success with extended schedules. Speaking in New Jersey in June of 2009, he praised the North Star Charter School, which has adopted both a longer day and an extended calendar. The school is in session 200 days, and each day is anywhere from an hour and a half to three hours longer than the regular public schools. He, too, pointed to the test scores of the students of North Star as evidence of the positive impact of the additional time spent in class.[8]

It is very likely that both Duncan and the president are impressed by the flexibility offered by charter schools. Most of these schools have the flexibility to increase their calendars without the obligation to negotiate the issue with a teachers union. Even though unions are working hard to organize the faculties of charter schools, most of these new schools are not yet unionized.

Like so many other educational innovations, research on the use of additional time in school has yielded a variety of results. *District Administration* reported in August of 2009 on the differences found in a survey done in Massachusetts and the Dade County public schools in Miami, Florida. In Massachusetts, where school time was increased by 300 hours per year, more teachers in the group with the extended day reported that "they have adequate time to cover the curriculum" than those teachers who were not part of the program.[9]

On the other hand, the same report found in Florida that the experiment was "problematic." Both students and teachers commented on "exhaustion from the extra hours per day, and many students stopped attending school altogether once summer vacation began at the district's other schools."[10]

Apparently, the experiment that is taking place in Massachusetts is indeed more positive. An article in the *Boston Globe* related a number of parental comments supporting the program. The same newspaper noted that praise was also forthcoming from President Obama, who saw it as a "model for national legislation." As of the 2009–2010 school year, twenty-two schools were participants in the state's Expanded Learning Time program. The article in the *Globe* reported that proficiency rates on state tests had increased "after just one year of the program."[11]

President Obama continued to highlight his initiative for additional instructional time in September of 2009. An Associated Press story about the president's remarks concerning more time in school included accounts of the reactions of several students. One fifth grader, Naknay Camara, commented that she enjoyed the four-week summer program at her school in Rockville, Maryland, and that she thinks the experience helped her "boost her grades from two Cs to the honor roll."[12]

On the other hand, she said that she doesn't want a longer day and if that happened, "I would walk straight out the door." Domonique Toombs agreed when she learned that she and her fellow students would spend "an extra three hours each day" in her sixth-grade classroom. Her comment was, "I was like, 'Wow, are you serious? . . . That's three more hours I won't be able to chill with my friends after school.'"[13]

The same Associated Press story also questioned the premise that children in the United States spend less time in school than students in other countries. It was noted that, "Kids in the U.S. spend more hours in school (1,146 instructional hours per year) than do kids in the Asian countries that persistently outscore the U.S. on math and science tests—Singapore (903), Taiwan

(1,050), Japan (1,005), and Hong Kong (1,013). That is despite the fact that Taiwan, Japan, and Hong Kong have longer school years (190–201 days) than does the U.S. (180 days)."[14]

While the administration presses for more time in class, the current economic crisis is pushing some school districts in the opposite direction. As noted earlier, in Hawaii the state legislature has actually reduced the time students are spending in school. Also, in Los Angeles, the head of the district proposed shortening the school year by six days in order to deal with the budget deficit. It was reported in *Education Week* that this "move would save the nation's second-largest school system a projected $90 million and an estimated 5,000 jobs." While admitting that the action would be drastic, Superintendent Ramon Cortines suggested that "the alternative could be bankruptcy for the district."[15]

In December of 2009, in Fairfax County, Virginia, a $650 million budget shortfall caused school officials to consider eliminating a modified school calendar that increased time in class at seven of their elementary schools. This option was being discussed despite the fact that the schools involved had achieved higher test scores, experienced a decrease in disciplinary referrals, and even had better attendance.[16]

In addition, teachers appeared to be happier and used fewer sick days. The district had also saved money by offering fewer summer remedial programs for the students in these schools. The same article that reported these positive results included comments on the current state of the research on the topic of extended class time. It stated, "Although a handful of schools using modified calendars have been around since the turn of the 20th century, the research on whether they boost student achievement or improve learning is muddy at best."[17]

Even though the early research might be less than convincing, the first national database of schools that have added learning time to their schedules released the results of a study in December of 2009, which suggested that "extra time might play a role in boosting middle and high school achievement." The research found that "sixth, seventh, eighth, and tenth graders in expanded-time schools outscored other students by 3–8 percentage points."[18]

Also included in the conclusions of the study was the fact that "schools that added the most time had better student performance in grades 7 and 10 than those that added less time." In defense of the study, it was pointed out that the extended-time schools "serve greater proportions of racial-minority and low-income students than do schools on regular schedules."[19]

As other districts debate the wisdom of changing their school calendars, the state of Massachusetts continues to lead the way. Even in these difficult economic times, Governor Deval Patrick has been able to maintain the program in his state. During the 2010 year, Massachusetts will have "22 so-called expanded learning time schools in 11 districts serving 12,000 students."[20] Whether other states and school districts will follow the lead of Massachusetts will depend in large part on whether or not the economy recovers to the point where states and districts can spend money on this initiative.

Another possibility is that federal funding could be given to selected schools that are willing to take on the task of changing their schedules. It is also possible that the federal government could mandate extra time in exchange for additional funding. Once again, it must be realized that this approach to improving education will not be universally popular in the United States. Just as with the issue of mayoral control of schools, President Obama will have to weigh carefully how much of his political capital he will use to push this initiative.

While he has a choice as to how far out in front he wishes to get on the issues of mayoral control and increases in school class time, he has no latitude in avoiding the challenge offered by the need to reauthorize the No Child Left Behind law. This very significant legislation is long overdue for reauthorization and Congress, as well as the entire educational establishment, is looking to the administration for leadership with this extremely difficult and politically explosive federal law.

NOTES

1. Brigid Schulte, "Year-Round School? My Kids Love It. Yours Will Too," *Washington Post*, 7 June 2009, www.washingtonpost.com/wp-dyn/content/article/2009/06/05/ar2009/06/05/ar2009060501971.html (accessed 3 February 2010).

2. "Length of School Day under Review across Nation," *Dallas News*, 24 February 2007, www.dallasnews.com/sharedcontent/dws/dn/education/stories/022507 dnnatschooldays.bcaeabd.html (accessed 11 February 2010).

3. Ibid.

4. Ibid.

5. Steven Thomma, "Obama Presses for Longer School Year," *Seattle Times*, 11 March 2009, seattletimes.nwsource.com/html/politics/2008838703_schools11.html (accessed 2 February 2010).

6. Ibid.

7. Steven Thomma, "Obama Urges Longer School Hours, Extended School Year," *American Policy Roundtable*, 10 March 2009, www.aproundtable.org/news .cfm?news_id=2419&issuecode=ed (11 February 2010).

8. "U.S. Education Secretary Takes His 'Listening and Learning' Tour to New Jersey," *U.S. Department of Education*, 5 June 2009, www2.ed.gov/news/pressre leases/2009/06/06052009.html (accessed 9 February 2010).

9. Don Parker-Burgard, "Longer School Day and Year Trials Yield Different Results," *District Administration*, August 2009, 10.

10. Ibid.

11. Lisa Kocian, "Looking for Lessons after a Long Day," *Boston Globe*, 9 August 2009, www.boston.com/news/local/articles/2009/08/09/year_of_extended_school _day_draws_mixed_reaction/ (accessed 3 February 2010).

12. "President Obama Wants to Keep Kids in School Longer: Extended Days, Weekend Hours, Shorter Summers," *New York Daily News*, 28 September 2009, www.nydailynews.com/news/national/2009/09/28/2009-09-28_president_obama _wants_to_keep_kids_in_school_longer_extended_days_weekends_hours_.html (accessed 2 February 2010).

13. Ibid.

14. Ibid.

15. "L.A. Superintendent Proposes Shortening School Year," *Education Week*, 15 February 2010, www.edweek.org/login.html?destination=http%3A%2F%2Fwww .edweek.org%2Ftm%2Farticles%2F2010%2F02%2F16%2Flashorterschoolyea r_ap.html (accessed 17 February 2010).

16. Brigid Schulte, "Putting the Brakes on 'Summer Slide,'" *Education Digest*, December 2009, vol. 75, iss. 4, 17–22.

17. Ibid.

18. Catherine Gewertz, "Study Eyes Effect of Extra Learning Time," *Education Week*, 7 December 2009, www.edweek.org/ew/articles/2009/12/09/14time.h29.html (accessed 11 December 2009).

19. Ibid.

20. "Mass. Renewing Push for Longer School Days," *Education Week*, 13 January 2010, www.edweek.org/ew/articles/2010/01/09/323042mlongerschooldays_ap.html (accessed 13 January 2010).

14

No Child Left Behind

The No Child Left Behind law was signed by President George W. Bush in January of 2002. It had been passed by Congress with strong bipartisan support. In the House of Representatives, the vote was 381 in favor with only 41 members against the bill. The margin in the Senate was just as one-sided, with 87 senators voting for the legislation and only 10 opposed.[1]

Along with President Bush, there were several members of Congress who were very instrumental in preparing the law and bringing about its passage. Perhaps the most prominent individuals were the present House minority leader, John A. Boehner, and the late Democratic senator from Massachusetts, Edward Kennedy.[2]

Actually, No Child Left Behind was the name given to the reauthorization of the Elementary Secondary Education Act, which was first passed in 1965 as part of President Lyndon Johnson's War on Poverty. During the presidential campaign in 2000, George W. Bush, who had been active in the field of education as governor of Texas, campaigned on the need for the federal government to bring about change in our schools. Candidate Bush talked frequently about how as governor he had been able to raise test scores in what had been labeled in the favorable press as the "Texas miracle." In speeches, he pointed especially to the gains made by black and Hispanic students in Texas.[3]

Some critics challenged whether there had actually been a Texas miracle. A study completed at Boston College pointed to the fact that at the same time Texas test scores were going up, the school dropout rate was also increasing, especially among minority students. The study implied that perhaps the scores had improved because schools were "pushing large numbers of kids out." Also, a Harvard research study concluded that the standards on the reading test had been lowered every year between 1995 and 1998.[4]

In any case, the education issue helped Bush in his campaign against Al Gore, who "really never found his voice on education." The Republican Party platform in the 2000 election included the following education initiatives:

- Private school vouchers
- Phonics-based reading programs
- Character education
- State curriculum standards
- High-stakes testing[5]

The fact that Republicans were interested in having the federal government become more active in the field of education was a change from the previous position held by the party. Conservative Republicans had for decades argued that schools should be the responsibility of state and local governments. In defending this traditional position, they pointed to the fact that education is not listed in the U.S. Constitution as a power that is delegated to the Congress and, therefore, for much of our nation's history, it was considered one of the powers reserved for the states. During the Reagan years, the party platform had actually called for abolishing the federal Department of Education, which had been established under President Carter.[6]

Still, as a result of the Nation at Risk Report issued by Reagan's Department of Education, as well as the programs of presidents George H. W. Bush and Bill Clinton, the federal role in education grew. Thus, President George W. Bush was merely continuing with an initiative begun by his predecessors. In talking about the purpose of the No Child Left Behind law in a speech in 2002, the president stated that the goal of the legislation was to make sure that "every child in every school must be performing at grade level in basic subjects that are key to all learning, reading and math."[7]

The legislation set the target year of 2014 to complete this task. An executive summary of the law published by the Department of Education outlines some of the major aspects of No Child Left Behind. They include the following:

- More flexibility for states and local educational agencies (LEA) in the use of federal education dollars. The bill gives "states and school districts unprecedented flexibility in the use of federal education funds in exchange for strong accountability for results."
- A stronger emphasis on reading, especially with our youngest children. A new Reading First grant program is included in the legislation. School

districts that are successful in gaining one of these grants will use the money to assist children in grades K–3 who are at risk of reading failure. The grants also provide professional development opportunities in the field of reading instruction for teachers of grades K–3.

- New Improving Teacher Quality state grants. These grants focus on providing assistance to schools in utilizing "scientifically based research to prepare, train, and recruit high-quality teachers."
- Assistance for states and local districts in providing safe, drug-free schools. "States must allow students who attend a persistently dangerous school or who are victims of violent crime at school to transfer to a safe school."[8]

While the initial reaction to the new law was often positive, within a short time it became the object of severe criticism. As school officials and the public became increasingly familiar with the hundreds of pages of the legislation, along with the complicated administrative guidelines prepared by the Department of Education, there were outcries of protest. By 2003, the Bush administration was on the defensive as it tried to enforce the legislation. Among the major problems was funding.[9]

The first year, there was a dramatic increase in federal aid made available to the schools, but in the years that followed, there was constant criticism that the president was failing to even recommend the funds necessary to carry out the mandates included in the law. Senator Kennedy would charge during the 2004 campaign, "President Bush thinks he is providing enough money for schools. Parents, teachers, and I don't."[10] As we have seen, candidate Obama in 2008 was also critical of President Bush for not providing the necessary money to bring about positive change in our public schools.

Money was only one of the problems with the law that emerged. Since its passage, the testing provisions have also come under fire. Because great importance is placed on the outcomes of the mandatory tests in language arts, math, and science, teachers and others have claimed that there is now excessive pressure on schools and teachers to "teach to the test."

For many, this has limited creative teaching methods and caused schools to deemphasize subjects such as social studies, the arts, and physical education. Because the Republican Party insisted that curriculum standards and tests be developed at the state level, other critics pointed to the uneven academic expectations among the states. They also charged that tests had been "dumbed down" so that most students would pass.

By 2007, polls were showing a decline in support for the No Child Left Behind law. One survey conducted by Phi Delta Kappa International found that "the public is evenly split on whether the law helps or hurts schools."

In support of the current initiative to create common standards and tests throughout the nation, an *Education Next* study reported that 73 percent of those surveyed in 2007 supported a change to federal standards and tests.[11]

The strongest opposition to the law seems now to be among professional educators. The Educational Testing Service found that 77 percent of teachers and 63 percent of school administrators hold a "staunchly negative" opinion of the law.[12] This opposition points to the fact that President Obama and Congress face a highly skeptical public as they begin the task of reauthorizing No Child Left Behind.

The fact that it was scheduled to be dealt with in 2007, and the Congress has yet to act, clearly demonstrates the difficulty faced in dealing with the issue. Because of a provision that maintains the present law in place until reauthorization occurs, it has been easy for the national leadership to delay taking action on reauthorization.

The same month that Obama was elected president, in November of 2008, the *Wall Street Journal* carried a story headlined, "Obama Is Expected to Put Education Overhaul on Back Burner." Citing the economic crisis as well as the other pressing issues, the article suggested that "at least early in his term" there will be "more about tinkering than about bold change."[13] Still, during his first month in office there were those who believed that "even in these difficult times, the education of America's youth deserves attention. President-elect Barack Obama must make it a priority to figure out what to do with the No Child Left Behind law."[14]

In 2009, the law remained in the news, even if it was in a debate about a new name for the legislation. Secretary Duncan agreed that a change would be a good thing. He was quoted in the *New York Times* as saying, "Let's rebrand it. . . . Give it a new name." The original title of the law was borrowed from a phrase used by children's advocate Marian Wright Edelman. Her new suggestion was to relabel it the "Quality Education for All Children Act." Others saw the idea of a new name as an opportunity for humor. An Internet blog set up for suggestions received the following entries, among many others:

- All American Children Are Above Average Act
- Mental Asset Recovery Plan
- Act to Help Children Read Gooder
- Pick Up the Children We Left Behind Act
- Rearranging the Deck Chairs Act
- Teach to the Test Act
- Could We Start Again, Please Act
- No Child Left Untested Act[15]

The *New York Times* carried another story about the law in April of 2009. Journalist Sam Dillon saw clues emerging from the administration that suggested it would be using the reauthorization issue "to toughen requirements on topics like teacher quality and academic standards and to intensify its focus on helping failing schools." The author went on to predict that "the law's testing requirements may evolve, but will certainly not disappear. And the federal role in education policy, once a state and local matter, is likely to grow." Secretary Duncan was quoted in the same article as saying that with the Race to the Top funding, the administration was "laying the foundation for where we want to go with N.C.L.B. reauthorization."[16]

During the spring of 2009, conflicting reports were published concerning the effectiveness of No Child Left Behind. A study by UCLA's Civil Rights Project found that "the basic assumptions of the law are not working and may well be making things worse." The authors went on to claim:

NCLB is failing on three fronts. First, there is little evidence that high stakes accountability under NCLB works. It has not improved student achievement and the sanctions have had limited effects in producing real improvement. The law also is not very good at accurately identifying schools needing improvement and far outstrips the ability of states to intervene effectively in the schools it sanctions. Third, the law has failed to connect in a meaningful way to the educators who must implement it—They do not see the accountability goals as realistic and consider the sanctions to be misguided and counterproductive for improving schools.[17]

A month later, in May, the *Washington Post* discussed a report outlining a new study done by the National Assessment of Educational Progress. This research found that "students at ages 9 and 13 did significantly better on 2008 tests than their counterparts of the early 1970s." That was the good news, but the same study noted that "the scores of seventeen-year-olds stayed alarmingly flat over 35 years."[18]

The gap between minority students and white Anglo-Saxon students had shrunk since 1971, but between 2004 and 2008 it did not change significantly. Even so, "black and Hispanic students of all age groups made greater gains in math than white students since 1973." One other interesting aspect of the study was that it appeared that "the emphasis on reading and math—contrary to the hypothesis of some critics—helped students to do well in other subjects such as science and history."[19]

On March 22, 2010, there was additional good news for those supporting the approach contained in the No Child Left Behind law. *Education Week* reported that "students in the nation's urban school districts have improved markedly in mathematics and reading proficiency as measured both on state

exams and the National Assessment of Educational Progress, according to a
new report by the Washington-based Council of the Great City Schools." The
council's executive director, Michael D. Casserly, was quoted as saying that
"the scores signal to me that we have a good handle on what's working in the
cities and where we need to go."[20]

While urban scores might have improved some, a *Washington Post*
article commenting on the overall impact of the law on test scores was
headlined, "NAEP Reading Scores: Bad News Was Sadly Predictable."
The story began with the statement, "Anybody paying attention over the
past eight years to the implementation of No Child Left Behind will not be
surprised that it failed to do what it was chiefly aimed at accomplishing:
Improving reading scores."[21]

In a recent report from the National Assessment of Educational Progress
(NAEP), which has been called the "nation's report card," it was noted that
fourth-grade reading scores stalled after the law took effect in 2002. There
was a slight increase in 2007, but they "stalled again in 2009." Eighth-grade
scores have shown "no real gain over the seven-year span when NCLB was
in high gear."[22]

Because of these discouraging results, there have been many suggestions
for improving NCLB. For example, an *Education Week* article written by
Gary W. Phillips argued that the biggest problem facing our schools was what
he called the "Lake Wobegon delusion." Using Garrison Keillor's comment
about the people in his town where everyone is above average, Phillips speaks
of the tendency of parents to believe that "everything is OK with my child in
my school, and it is everyone and everywhere else that is failing."[23]

This occurs because the state standards and tests vary so greatly. His argument is that allowing states to develop their own curriculum standards and
testing leads most people to believe that their children are, for the most part,
doing fine. His answer is that "knowledge is the antidote to the Lake Wobegon delusion, and once the veil of ignorance is lifted and parents and teachers
find out how their students and schools stack up against others, we will finally
begin to have true educational accountability."[24]

Perhaps one of the most important sources offering advice to the president
was the Alliance for Excellent Education, which called for including the following in any revision of the No Child Left Behind law:

- Establish college and career readiness as the common goal for all students.
- Ensure meaningful accountability for high school outcomes designed
  around common indicators of college and career readiness and high
  school graduation.

- Replace the current flawed, one-size-fits-all school improvement process with requirements for state- and district-led systems that are differentiated and data driven, and prioritize addressing the lowest-performing schools.
- Support strategies that are necessary to implement high school improvement at a much larger scale, including districtwide efforts, maximizing the role of entities outside of the school system with expertise to contribute.
- Build the capacity of the system to implement innovative solutions— bold approaches to teaching and learning, school organization, and system structure that result in higher expectations and achievement for all students.
- Provide new funding for the implementation of innovative solutions to address low-performing high schools.[25]

This report identified many of the proposals that would be made by the Obama administration as part of its reauthorization plan.

A major negative note in the effort to reauthorize No Child Left Behind was sounded by Diane Ravitch, a respected educational historian. In an article in *Education Week* in June of 2009, titled "Time to Kill 'No Child Left Behind,'" Ravitch began what would become a year-long campaign against No Child Left Behind, as well as other aspects of the Obama program. This opposition represented a dramatic change in Ravitch's educational views.[26]

As one of the people who helped develop and champion the law, she has come to believe that it has failed. Her new position is based on her view that "the achievement gap between white and minority students has hardly budged over the past decade." She continues to point out publicly that while "average scores are up for 9-year-olds and 13-year-olds in reading and mathematics between 2004 and 2008, the rate of improvement is actually smaller than it was in the previous period measured, from 1999 to 2004."[27]

In March of 2010, Ravitch was in the news again when she published a book titled *The Death and Life of the Great American School System: How Testing and Choice Are Undermining Education*. The purpose of the book is to explain why she has done an "about-face on charter schools, school choice, and other market-oriented reform strategies in education." She also makes clear that she no longer supports the No Child Left Behind Act. Despite her early enthusiastic support of the law, she now believes that it "ought to be ended rather than mended."[28]

The book quickly gained the support of Randi Weingarten, the president of the American Federation of Teachers, especially because it opposes what she sees as the "current attempts to tie teachers' pay to their students' test-score gains," which she describes as "teacher bashing." The timing of the publication of this book could not be worse for the Obama administration, as it comes while Congress is debating the administration's proposals for reauthorizing No Child Left Behind.[29]

Not only is the president being criticized by Ravitch, but there are also a number of members of Congress who are questioning the validity of the law. The *Washington Post* reported in July of 2009 that a number of Republicans are less than enthusiastic about the challenge of reauthorizing No Child Left Behind. The article pointed to the fact that the new ranking House Republican on the Education and Labor Committee, John D. Kline (Minnesota), did not vote for the original legislation.[30]

Like Ravitch, Kline too wishes to give back to the states "maximum latitude." He has expressed the opinion that "I'm not looking to tweak No Child Left Behind. . . . As far as I'm concerned, we ought to go in and look at the whole thing." The article went on to suggest that "Kline and a growing number of like-minded members of his party devoted to local control of schools are likely to complicate Obama's efforts to build a broad bipartisan coalition for the next generation of education reform."[31]

It is not only members of Congress who are questioning the value of No Child Left Behind. The results of a Phi Delta Kappa study found that 67 percent of the registered Republicans surveyed believe that the law was either hurting or making no difference in their community. If that conveys less than enthusiastic support, the results of those Democrats who were part of the study found that 78 percent felt that the law was hurting or making no difference in their schools. Even though much of the law is somewhat unpopular, the idea that common tests should be given in every state was supported by a 2-to-1 ratio.[32]

Even with the public divided in their opinions concerning No Child Left Behind, the administration began to become active during the fall of 2009, by gradually releasing information about the positions to be taken by the administration during the reauthorization debate. Speaking to a diverse group of education interest groups, Secretary Duncan recognized the fear of many that the federal government was trying to take over public education.[33]

He made the point that "people want support from Washington, but not interference. They want accountability, but not oversight. They want national leadership, but not at the expense of local control." He further suggested that "the biggest problem with NCLB is that it doesn't encourage high enough standards. In fact, it inadvertently encourages states to lower them. The net effect is that we are lying to children and parents by telling kids they are succeeding when they are not." In this same speech, he introduced the idea that our primary concern as a nation should be "focused on student achievement, high school graduation, and college."[34]

By the fall of 2009, it was apparent that there would be dissenters no matter what proposals the administration put forward in the field of education. *U.S. News & World Report* chronicled this division in an article titled "No Child Left Behind and the Brewing Fight over Education." It noted that the bipartisan coalition that had supported the law in 2001 was gone. Part of the problem seemed to be that the Republicans were looking forward to the 2010 elections and were "not inclined to enable victories for Democrats."[35]

Because of the many unresolved issues regarding the law, an article in the *New York Times* in January of 2010 predicted in a headline: "A Rewrite of Nation's Main Education Law Will Be Hard This Year."[36] Despite the apparent difficulties, on the first day in February of 2010, President Obama began to publicly announce the outline of his plans for updating No Child Left Behind. He made it clear that the Adequate Yearly Progress, or AYP approach, to judging schools "would be replaced with a new metric that would measure student progress toward readiness for college or a career."[37]

A month later, the president announced additional details of his plan. He noted that he would ask for $49.7 billion in discretionary spending increases for education in the upcoming budget. This was an increase of $3.5 billion for the 2010 fiscal year. The budget request would also include an additional $34.9 billion for Pell grants. The administration would also seek a third round of competitive grants under the Race to the Top format, and $2.2 billion would be used to "intervene in failing schools," encourage charter schools, and improve teacher recruiting and training.[38]

Almost immediately, as the ideas were introduced, the debate on the proposals began. The "standard of college and career readiness" raised many questions because it was not yet clearly defined. Others were concerned about "what sanctions would apply . . . for schools that are missing the law's achievement targets." There were also questions about the "teacher effectiveness" section in the proposal. The issue was potentially controversial because of the wording that said teachers would be judged "in significant part on student learning." To some, this meant that teachers would be evaluated in large part by the results of student testing.[39]

By the end of February 2010, the outline of the administration's plan for reauthorization was becoming clear, and activity to move it forward was beginning to occur. On February 18, a group of senior House Republicans and Democrats announced that they would begin to "team up to rewrite the No Child Left Behind education law." At the same time, it was noted that "many analysts" agreed that "time was growing short for the passage of a major education bill before the midterm election."[40]

In a speech to the nation's governors, Secretary Duncan sought to justify the new goal of providing academic standards that are "college and career ready." The importance of this element of the proposal was made clear by the Department of Education when it announced that "only states that adopt these standards would be eligible to receive Title I funding."[41]

Even with the announcement of the bipartisan cooperation that was to characterize the efforts at reauthorization, one observer suggested that "the politically poisonous atmosphere in Congress . . . poses a mortal threat to any significant piece of legislation." As formal hearings opened in the House of Representatives, several issues appeared to be creating problems. Although it was clear that testing would remain an important way to measure academic progress, there seemed to be many questions about the effort to abolish the Adequate Yearly Progress formula. There was also the very important issue of whether or not the national curriculum standards, and possibly tests, would replace those that are currently used by the states.[42]

The National School Boards Association quickly expressed their concern about the possibility of federal standards. They were "worried" that the national government was "stepping on what has been a state and local issue." Supporters of the president's plan pointed out, in regard to common standards, that "states could opt not to join in a common standards effort and instead work with higher education institutions to draft rigorous, college-and-career-ready standards."[43]

Advocates of states rights appear to be worried about the fact that even if states develop their own standards, they would have to be approved by the federal Department of Education. Although forty-eight states have entered into the effort to develop common standards, it is too early to tell whether all of them will adopt what is agreed upon.[44]

There are other aspects of the administration's proposal that fundamentally alter the current law. The president is recommending that "more than a dozen discrete programs" be combined "into three broader, competitive funds focused on 'effective teaching and learning' across academic-content areas." Specifically, the new classifications would center on "literacy, the STEM fields of science, technology, engineering, and mathematics, and a final catchall category dubbed a 'well-rounded education.'" Another major change in the president's approach is an increased emphasis on competitive grants, which will be based on the Race to the Top model.[45]

While the competitive grants might have strong support, members in the House have already demonstrated "qualms about aspects of the administration's fiscal 2011 budget proposal." The leader of the Republican majority on the Education and Labor Committee, John Kline of Minnesota, is worried that "putting the federal government in charge of what is taught and tested in the classroom would be a radical departure from this country's approach to education." Even with such comments, Democrat George Miller of California, the chairperson of the committee, still is hopeful that a reauthorization plan could be completed in 2010.[46]

The Senate began its own hearings in March of 2010. Secretary Duncan was one of the first witnesses called before the committee. The discussion in the first Senate hearing "centered around big ideas, like education's role in the overall economy, as opposed to nitty-gritty details." Additional hearings will deal with standards, assessments, school turnaround, teachers and leaders, and special populations.[47]

In his weekly radio address on March 13, 2010, the president addressed another of the controversial aspects of the current legislation. The provision in question was the 2014 deadline which, under the law, is the date by which all students are supposed to be proficient in reading and math. The president implied that this idea would "essentially go away under the department's blueprint."[48]

While teachers would certainly applaud the idea of abandoning what they feel is an unrealistic deadline, both major unions have already expressed concerns about the administration's plans. The largest teachers union, the National Education Association, is unhappy about the "preservation of annual testing, even though the law would no longer specify interventions for the majority of schools." The American Federation of Teachers has not formally reacted to the testing provision, but union president Randi Weingarten has been quoted as saying that the administration's proposals place "100 percent of the responsibility on teachers and gives them zero percent authority."[49]

In March of 2010, a headline story caused a new rift between President Obama and the teachers unions. When a Rhode Island school district fired all of the teachers and administrators in a failing high school, the president and Secretary Duncan spoke as if they approved of the action. The fact is that the administration's own plan includes such an option as one of the ways for dealing with the poorest-performing schools. Dennis Van Roekel, president of the National Education Association, reacted to the issue by saying, "It's just not a solution to say, 'Let's get rid of half the staff.' . . . If there's a high-crime neighborhood, you don't fire the police officers. This is a huge issue for us."[50]

Even if this is true, it must be noted that the drastic measures alluded to in the administration's plan would only be considered in approximately five thousand of the lowest-performing districts. Currently, there are 31,737 schools that missed the law's testing goals last year.[51] While fewer schools might be involved, both unions have complained that there is "too much 'scapegoating' and not enough 'collaboration' in the proposal."[52] Charles Barone, a former aid of Rep. George Miller, has observed that the opposition of unions might result in less Democratic support in the Congress.[53]

In fact, in April of 2010, the National Education Association released its own plan for reauthorization. In this 170-page document, the organization called for "far fewer standardized tests." Instead, the group suggested assessing student growth using "nonstandardized" methods such as portfolios. Under their plan, "schools would be judged on growth toward an annual performance target and on their progress in closing achievement gaps. Schools that fell below the 5th percentile on one of those indicators would be subject to school improvement, which would be locally designed and involve the input of external school review teams."[54]

The plan also differed from the president's blueprint in that it did not endorse the idea of performance-pay for teachers. The other major difference was that both the NEA and the AFT oppose efforts to assess teachers on the basis of student test scores. It will be a major challenge for the administration to find ways to gain union support for its reauthorization plan.[55] If Democratic votes are lost due to the opposition of teachers unions, the administration will be forced "to find more votes within the Republican caucus." It is possible that some "Republicans will find much to like in the blueprint."[56]

Even with some Republican help, there will be problems in gaining majority support for the administration's plans. An editorial in the *New York Times* on March 17, 2010, agreed that the president's plans for amending No Child Left Behind included many "good ideas." Still, it cautioned that whether the proposal "will strengthen or weaken the program will depend on how the administration fleshes out the missing details—and how Congress rewrites the law."[57]

The *Times* believed that it was "sensible" to make available "financial rewards and greater flexibility to schools and districts that show large improvements in student learning." The editorial was most enthusiastic about the goal of developing "new strategies for getting states to measure, develop and improve the effectiveness of teachers, principals and programs in teacher preparation."[58]

While it would seem that public opinion is ready for major changes in the No Child Left Behind law, it remains to be seen if Congress is capable of arriving at a consensus prior to the elections in November of 2010. Given the track record with the health care issue, it is difficult to be confident. Because there are so many major decisions to be made, it is very possible that reauthorization will be left to a new Congress in 2011. In any case, by the spring of 2010, the education agenda of the Obama administration was in place.

The purpose of the final chapter will be to summarize the educational goals of President Obama and to compare them with the educational goals of those who have a different vision.

NOTES

1. William Hayes, *No Child Left Behind: Past, Present, and Future* (Lanham, Md.: Rowman & Littlefield Education, 2008), 13.

2. Elisabeth Bumiller, "Focus on Home Front, Bush Signs Education Bill," *New York Times*, 9 January 2002.

3. Andrew Rudalevige, "The Politics of No Child Left Behind," *Education Next*, vol. 3, no. 4 (2003), www.hoover.org/publications/ednext/3346601.html (accessed 16 March 2010).

4. David Schuman, *American Schools, American Teachers* (Upper Saddle River, N.J.: Pearson, 2004), 244.

5. L. Dean Webb, *The History of American Education* (Upper Saddle River, N.J.: Pearson, 2006), 360.

6. "The Politics of No Child Left Behind."

7. Mary E. Williams, ed., *Education: Opposing Viewpoints* (Detroit: Thomson Gale, 2005), 156.

8. U.S. Department of Education, "No Child Left Behind: Executive Summary," January 2001, www.ed.gov/nclb/overview/intro/execsumm.html?exp=0 (accessed 10 March 2010).

9. "Bush Makes Money, Touts Education," *Inside Politics*, 6 January 2004, CNN .com, www.cnn.com/2004/allpolitics/01/06/elec04.prez.bush.fundraising.ap/index .html (accessed 16 March 2010).

10. Ibid.

11. William G. Howell, Martin R. West, and Paul E. Peterson, "What Americans Think about Their Schools: The 2007 *Education Next*–PEPG Survey," *Education Next*, vol. 7, no. 4 (2007), www.hoover.org/publications/ed/next/8769517.html (accessed 16 March 2010).

12. Howard Blume, "Parents, Educators Split on What to Do with No Child Left Behind," *Los Angeles Times*, 25 June 2007, www.districtadministration.com/news summary.aspx?news=yes&postid=19397 (accessed 16 March 2010).

13. Robert Tomosho and John Hechinger, "Obama Is Expected to Put Education Overhaul on Back Burner," *Wall Street Journal*, 11 November 2008, online.wsj.com/ article/SB1226322505351663.html (accessed 1 September 2009).

14. "Editorial: No Child Left Behind," *Philadelphia Inquirer*, 16 January 2009, www.philly.com/inquirer/opinion/20090116_editorial_no _child_left_behind.html (accessed 27 April 2007).

15. Sam Dillon, "Rename Law? No Wisecrack Is Left Behind," *New York Times*, 22 February 2009, www.nytimes.com/2009/02/23/education/23child.html (accessed 27 April 2009).

16. Sam Dillon, "Education Standards Likely to See Toughening," *New York Times*, 14 April 2009, www.nytimes.com/2009/04/15/education/15educ.html (accessed 27 April 2009).

17. Gary Orfield, "Press Release: New Study by UCLA's Civil Rights Projects: NCLB Ignores What We Know about School Change and Is Motivated by Politics," *UCLA, The Civil Rights Project*, 22 April 2009, www.civilrightsproject.ucla.edu/news/pressreleases/pressrelease20090422-nclb.html (accessed 24 April 2009).

18. "What Test Results Suggest," *Washington Post*, 10 May 2009, www.washingtonpost.com/wp-dyn/content/article/2009/05/09/ar2009050902142.html (accessed 11 May 2009).

19. Ibid.

20. Dakarai I. Aarons, "Big-City Test Scores on Rise, Report Says," *Education Week*, 22 March 2010, www.edweek.org/ew/articles/2010/03/22/27odds.h29.html?tkn=ZZNF8mSU4AkSeh%2B%2Fr0RSHVX7kcy3EhU7%2Fu3v&cmp=clp-edweek (accessed 22 March 2010).

21. Valerie Strauss, "NAEP Reading Scores: Bad News Was Sadly Predictable," *Washington Post*, 24 March 2010, voices.washingtonpost.com/answer-sheet/reading/naep-reading-scores-bad-news-w.html (accessed 25 March 2010).

22. Ibid.

23. Gary W. Phillips, "How to Fix No Child Left Behind," *Education Week*, 11 May 2009, www.edweek.org/ew/articles/2009/05/13/31phillips_ep.h28.html (accessed 10 July 2009).

24. Ibid.

25. "Reinventing the Federal Role in Education: Supporting the Goal of College and Career Readiness for All Students," *Alliance for Excellent Education*, July 2009, 1–2.

26. Diane Ravitch, "Time to Kill 'No Child Left Behind,'" *Education Week*, 8 June 2009, www.edweek.org/ew/articles/2009/06/04/33ravitch_ep.h28.html (accessed 15 June 2009).

27. Ibid.

28. Debra Viadero, "In New Book, Ravitch Recants Long-Held Beliefs," *Education Week*, 4 March 2010, www.edweek.org/ew/articles/2010/03/04/24ravitch_ep.h29.html (accessed 12 March 2010).

29. Ibid.

30. Nick Anderson, "GOP Leaving 'No Child' Behind," *Washington Post*, 13 July 2009, www.washingtonpost.com/wp-dyn/content/article/2009/07/12/ar2009071202298.html (accessed 20 July 2009).

31. Ibid.

32. Dakarai I. Aarons, "Obama School Ideas Getting Good Grades," *Education Week*, vol. 29, no. 2, 2 September 2009, 7.

33. Transcript, "Ed Sec Duncan's Speech on NCLB," *Washington Post*, 23 September 2009, voices.washingtonpost.com/answer-sheet/no-child-left-behind/transcript-prepared-remarks-fo.html (accessed 22 October 2009).

34. Ibid.

35. Andrew J. Rotherham, "No Child Left Behind and the Brewing Fight over Education," *U.S. News & World Report*, 10 November 2009, www.usnews.com/articles/opinion/2009/11/10/no-child-left-behind-and-the-brewing-fight-over-education.html (accessed 13 November 2009).

36. Sam Dillon, "Experts Say a Rewrite of Nation's Main Education Law Will Be Hard This Year," *New York Times*, 28 January 2010, www.nytimes.com/2010/01/29/education/29child.html (accessed 5 February 2010).

37. Alyson Klein, "Debate Heats Up over Replacing AYP Metric in ESEA," *Education Week*, 5 February 2010, www.edweek.org/ew/articles/2010/02/05/21eseaweb_ep.h29.html (accessed 5 February 2010).

38. Sam Dillon, "Administration Outlines Proposed Changes to 'No Child' Law," *New York Times*, 1 February 2010, www.nytimes.com/2010/02/02/education/02child.html?hpw (accessed 3 February 2010).

39. "Debate Heats Up over Replacing AYP Metric in ESEA."

40. Nick Anderson, "Lawmakers to Launch Bipartisan Effort to Rewrite No Child Left Behind," *Washington Post*, 18 February 2010, www.washingtonpost.com/wp-dyn/content/article/2010/02/17/ar2010021705195.html (accessed 3 March 2010).

41. Lesli Maxwell, "ESEA Plan Could Tether Title I to College-and-Career Standards," *Education Week*, 21 February 2010, blogs.edweek.org/edweek/state_edwatch/2010/02/as_part_of_the_obama.html (accessed 22 February 2010).

42. Michele McNeil, "House Committee to Hold Hearings on New ESEA," *Education Week*, 22 February 2010, www.edweek.org/ew/articles/2010/02/24/22esea.h29.html (accessed 22 February 2010).

43. Alyson Kelin, "Not Everyone Loves White House Title I/Standards Proposal," *Education Week*, 23 February 2010, blogs.edweek.org/edweek/ . . ./not_everyone_loves_white_house.html (accessed 24 February 2010).

44. Ibid.

45. Erik W. Robelen, "Obama Wants to Consolidate Curriculum Programs," *Education Week*, 26 February 2010, www.edweek.org/ew/articles/2010/03/03/23curriculum_ep.h29.html (accessed 2 March 2010).

46. Alyson Kelin, "House Panel Questions Duncan on ESEA and Budget," *Education Week*, 3 March 2010, www.edweek.org/ew/articles/2010/03/03/24duncan.h29.html (accessed 4 March 2010).

47. Alyson Klein, "Senate Education Committee Holds First ESEA Hearing," *Education Week*, 9 March 2010, blogs.edweek.org/edweek/.../senate_education_committee_hol.html (accessed 10 March 2010).

48. Alyson Kelin, "Administration Unveils ESEA Renewal Blueprint," *Education Week*, 13 March 2010, ww.edweek.org/ew/articles/2010/03/13/25esea.h29.html (accessed 15 March 2010).

49. Stephen Sawchuk, "Teachers, Unions, and the NCLB 'Blueprint,'" *Education Week*, 15 March 2010, blogs.edweek.org/edweek/teacherbeat/2010/03/teachers_unions_and_the_nclb_b.html (accessed 16 March 2010).

50. Sam Dillon, "Array of Hurdles Awaits New Education Agenda," *New York Times*, 15 March 2010, www.nytimes.com/2010/03/16/education/16educ.html?hpw (accessed 17 March 2010).

51. Ibid.

52. "Teachers, Unions, and the NCLB 'Blueprint.'"

53. Alyson Klein, "Interest Turns to ESEA Plan's Chances of Passing," *Education Week*, 15 March 2010, www.edweek.org/ew/articles/2010/03/15/27eseareax.h29 .html (accessed 16 March 2010).

54. Stephen Sawchuk, "NEA Plan for Rewriting NCLB Departs from Obama's," *Education Week*, 13 April 2010, www.edweek.org/ew/articles/2010/04/13/29nea .h29.html (accessed 13 April 2010).

55. Ibid.

56. "Interest Turns to ESEA Plan's Chances of Passing."

57. "Mr. Obama and No Child Left Behind," *New York Times*, 17 March 2010, www.nytimes.com/2010/03/18/opinion/18thu1.html?ref=opinion (accessed 18 March 2010).

58. Ibid.

III

THE FUTURE

15

The Agenda

It has been the purpose of this book to seek to identify the factors that have influenced the views of Barack Obama in the field of education. With this background, it became the goal to highlight the actions and proposals of Obama since becoming president. Despite the many issues that faced him in 2009, he has been very active in his efforts to improve the educational opportunities for the students in this country. The initiatives he has promoted thus far provide a clear outline of the future educational agenda of his administration.

Beginning with the use of the economic stimulus package to save the jobs of teachers, he has demonstrated leadership in promoting the educational objectives that he supports. With the Race to the Top, the president used federal money to mandate several of his favorite approaches to improving our schools. This was done by using money to require some states to lift the limits that they had placed on the number of charter schools and to also repeal any legislation that prohibited the use of student test results as one of the ways to evaluate teachers.

Other areas in which the administration has been active include the following:

- Support for early childhood education
- Involvement and leadership in the preparation of national curriculum standards
- Speaking out in favor of adding additional instructional time to school schedules
- Active campaigning for the spread of the charter school movement

- Major initiatives in higher education and support for reform of teacher education programs
- Seeking to sustain a movement to pay teachers based on their performance in the classroom
- Mayoral control of urban school districts

The single most significant educational issue facing President Obama is the reauthorization of the No Child Left Behind legislation. On March 13, 2010, the administration introduced its blueprint for the revision of the law. One of the most important aspects of the plan is for states to be required to "adopt standards that ensure students are ready for college or a career rather than grade-level proficiency—the focus of the current law."[1]

The proposal also encourages states "to use subjects other than reading and mathematics as part of their measurements for meeting federal goals." In addition, there is a $4 billion increase in federal education spending, much of which will be used for competition among the states for grant money. This is a change from the current system of allotting funds, which is based on a specific formula.[2]

The blueprint forces states that accept Title I aid for disadvantaged students to articulate definitions of "effective teacher, effective principal, highly effective teacher, and highly effective principal." These categories will be "based in significant part on student academic growth." The reporting requirements called for also become more demanding for both districts and states. "At least every two years," the federal government would require from each school information concerning the "distribution of effective teachers and principals; rates of teacher and principal absenteeism; teacher-retention rates; educators' level of experience; and teacher-survey data on the level of support and working conditions. States also would be required to report on the effectiveness of their teacher-preparation programs."[3]

The many far-reaching proposals that have been put forward by the Obama administration have created a program that could be considered in the education field to be comparable with Franklin Roosevelt's New Deal. While Roosevelt was attempting to solve an economic crisis, Obama is trying to deal with a similar dilemma in the field of education. In many ways, this was also true of Lyndon Johnson's initiative to wipe out poverty.

In both of these historic programs, the presidents were willing to try a variety of approaches and they were probably aware that some would be more helpful than others. Like President Obama's initiatives in education, not all of the New Deal or the War on Poverty could be justified by research. It is also true, as with any reform movement, that there will be serious opposition from many sources.

Perhaps the most important groups that must be convinced of the merits of the president's plans are the two major teachers unions. While their concerns with the blueprint have already surfaced, the president has also been praised for his willingness to upset the unions. A columnist writing in the *Seattle Times* noted that "the right accuses Barack Obama of dragging the country way left, and the left calls him gutless. The president is proving both of them wrong." The editorial went on to say, "From under the mild-mannered exterior has recently emerged a man of steel. . . . He's tackling problems that conservatives say only they have the gumption to fix. And he's doing it at the risk of offending important Democratic constituencies."[4]

Besides the likely opposition of teachers unions, there is a second factor that could easily curtail the president's plans: Unless there is a significant economic recovery, states and school districts will be spending most of their time and money trying to deal with a lack of financial aid. The stimulus bill helped "to cushion the recession's impact on schools and [helped to] fuel an economic recovery, but new studies show that many states will spend all, or nearly all, that is left" of this aid by the end of the 2009–2010 school year.[5]

To deal with this problem there will need to be either a significant reduction in school budgets or an influx of new money. The three primary sources of funding for schools include local property taxes, state aid, and federal aid. In a weak economy, it is unlikely that communities will be willing to raise either property taxes or sales taxes. With both the federal and state governments facing increasingly high levels of debt, it will become difficult for any political leader to gain support for additional school funding.

The *Washington Post* reported in February of 2010 that "in many hard-hit districts more teacher layoffs, larger class sizes, smaller paychecks, fewer electives and extracurricular activities, and decimated summer school programs" have been included in their 2010–2011 budgets. The same article included the fact that "41 states face midyear budget shortfalls totaling $35 billion."[6] Overall, it has been predicted that nationwide there could be 275,000 school employees laid off during the 2010–2011 school year. This number is close to the estimated 300,000 jobs saved as a result of the stimulus program.[7]

As a result, the administration is supporting legislation that will provide $23 billion to lessen the effect of teacher layoffs that have already been announced for the 2010–2011 school year.[8] With many Americans extremely worried about the federal deficit, the possibility of Congress granting administration requests for large increases in federal aid to education are also very much in doubt. This situation will worsen if the Democratic Party loses a significant number of seats in the 2010 Congressional election.

Along with the opposition of some members of both parties, as well as the teachers unions, a number of voices within the educational community have begun to speak out against the Obama agenda for education. For example, Thomas Hatch published an article in *Education Week* titled "Four Flawed Assumptions of School Reform." He identified what for him are the "flawed assumptions":

- We have the capacity to significantly improve the performance of all students; we just need to put in place the goals and incentives that will encourage teachers and schools to do it.
- If a school makes some improvements and hits some performance targets at one time, it has the capacity to continue to make meaningful improvements in instruction over time.
- Competition for students will lead to innovation and improve performance in many schools.
- The way to improve the system as a whole is to "scale up" the successes of individual programs and schools around the country.[9]

Hatch believes that all of these assumptions are wrong and that "in education, even the most successful school networks and model programs only work in some places, under some circumstances" and that the effort "to scale up successful schools and programs has to be accompanied by a concerted effort to create more favorable economic, organizational, social, and political conditions that will give all schools a better chance to make significant improvements."[10]

Others would agree with Hatch that the social and economic problems of so many Americans are a major factor in the failure of a significant number of our public schools. An article by Jim Taylor in *Psychology Today* suggests that the primary need is to attempt to reduce "the achievement gap that exists between lower- and higher-income students." For Taylor, the problem of public education in America cannot be changed by school reform alone, but rather requires changing the lives of poor school children.[11]

He disagrees with an observation made by Secretary Duncan, who said, "When I was in Chicago, people used to warn me that we could never fix schools until we ended poverty. . . . But I reject this idea that demography is destiny. Despite challenges at home . . . I know that every child can learn and thrive." Taylor suggests that "decades and billions of dollars would argue otherwise." He believes that although we have been attempting to reduce the achievement gap, it will not be totally possible until we deal with the poverty and difficult family life of so many of our children.[12]

In his syndicated column, Clarence Page shared some statistics relating to families in our society. He noted that in 2008, 41 percent of American births were to single mothers. This was a change from 28 percent in 1990. For black mothers, the rate is 72 percent and for Hispanic mothers, it is 53 percent. Page argued that this trend "does not bode well for kids. Traditional marriage is better for kids emotionally, academically, and economically."[13]

He also noted that in the book *The Audacity of Hope*, Barack Obama wrote that "children 'living with single mothers are five times more likely to be poor than children in two-parent homes. . . . And the evidence suggests that on average, children who live with their biological mother and father do better than those who live in stepfamilies or with cohabiting partners.'"[14] Along with the need to solve the social problems facing our children, there are others who have raised concerns about the Obama agenda for educational reform.

Among the current critics is another well-known education writer. John Goodlad, the author of three dozen books on education, including a best seller titled *A Place Called School*, has indicated in the *New York Times* that the good news is that No Child Left Behind will soon be history, but the proposed reforms are "déjà vu all over again—been there, done that." For him, we are merely "tinkering, one more time, toward an ill-defined utopia." He is extremely worried about "narrowing of pedagogy to simply drilling for tests." Goodlad believes that "we do not need schools for this. It is training, not education." The goal must be to assist each student to become "a unique human being whose responsibility is to make the most of oneself."[15]

Along the same line as Goodlad, Deborah Meier, a respected teacher, school administrator, and author, is very concerned about the continuation of the use of traditional tests to assess schools and teachers. For her, "the evaluative process should be treated less like the part of a driver's test where we complete a pen-and-paper exam, and more like the part where we actually get in a car and show what we can do on a real road with real traffic and real-time scenarios."[16]

This can be done using what is called "performance assessment." For Deborah Meier, such an approach "requires schools to invest in seven interrelated components: active learning; formative and summative documentation; strategies for correction action; multiple ways for students to express and exhibit learning; graduation-level performance tasks that are aligned with the school's learning standards; external evaluators of student work; and a focus on professional development." She asks the question, "Would we support a driving test that failed to test actual driving?"[17]

On the other side of the debate, there are those who have said that the Obama plan would reduce school accountability. Margaret Spellings, secretary of education under George W. Bush, has also publicly criticized the Obama plan for reforming schools. She has charged that "accountability has vanished. . . . Gone are today's requirements that schools make annual yearly progress. No longer would every school be responsible for improving the progress of its students. The administration's blueprint says that up to 90 percent of schools could escape accountability for the performance of all students."[18]

Not only does the president have people on both the left and the right second-guessing him, he has also been blamed by Wayne Au in the *Harvard Educational Review* for trying "to have his cake and eat it too: he is both for and against NCLB, critical of but not opposed to high-stakes testing, supportive of public charter schools, yet not necessarily private ones and in favor of both performance pay and teacher tenure. He is neither here nor there on any one issue. Or, put conversely, like a master of political quantum physics, Obama is both here and there on all of these issues at the same time."[19]

Of all of those opposing the president's educational agenda, perhaps the most influential is Diane Ravitch. A respected education historian, she was an early supporter of both No Child Left Behind and charter schools. In her new best-selling book *The Death and Life of the Great American School System: How Testing and Choice Are Undermining Education*, she writes that she now supports the repeal of the law she once praised, and she also wishes to discontinue the spread of charter schools.[20]

Unlike the president and the secretary of education, the college professor is a graduate of a traditional public school system. She is now devoted to the improvement of our neighborhood public schools, which she feels is a better alternative than the administration's preference for school choice.

One might wonder whether the fact that both Obama and Duncan are products of excellent private schools might have lessened their commitment to the neighborhood public school. In any case, Diane Ravitch is now opposed to "school choice, and other market-oriented reform strategies in education." At the same time, she is against any "endeavors designed to hold schools and teachers accountable for their students' test results." In her book, she suggests that the administration's agenda has been greatly influenced by a number of major foundations which are providing money for education reform. Specifically, she mentions the Bill and Melinda Gates Foundation.[21]

To support her new positions, she includes in her book evidence that questions the success of charter schools. She refers to not only test scores, but also the fact that they have not, as hoped, created significant new ideas for improving instruction in all public schools. Instead, she has hinted that they might become even a replacement school system.[22] Ravitch has also written that the administration's program of "incentives and sanctions may be right for business organizations, where the bottom line—profit—is the highest priority, but they are not right for schools."[23] It is instructive that Randi Weingarten, the president of the American Federation of Teachers, has expressed her agreement with many of Ravitch's arguments.

Even though Diane Ravitch's ideas are getting a great deal of attention from the media, she too has her critics. The former president of Teachers College at Columbia University, Arthur E. Levine, has written that "she has done more than anyone I can think of in America to drive home the message of accountability and charters and testing. . . . Now for her to suddenly conclude that she's been all wrong is extraordinary—and not very helpful." An acquaintance of Professor Ravitch, Chester E. Finn Jr., has been quoted as saying, "Diane says, 'Let's return to the old public school system,' and I say, 'Let's blow it up.'"[24]

Another observer, Brad C. Phillips, is also puzzled by Ravitch's dramatic change of opinion. He has raised the question, "How could what was all right five years ago be all wrong today?" For him, "Ravitch was mostly right then and is mostly right now. The problem isn't business principles, standards, and testing—it's how they are applied."[25]

Phillips writes that "our charge should be to help teachers work collaboratively, using business tools and data, to guide and fuel the magic of teaching. Without it, we're just guessing. And that's not right. So Diane Ravitch's ability to see problems from two sides is in fact a refreshing departure. We need to move off the poles and toward the middle. That's where the data and the ability of educators to take action to improve reside."[26]

If anyone can see problems from two sides, it is Barack Obama. Perhaps the criticisms of teachers and writers such as Diane Ravitch will lead the president and Congress "to the middle," where individual teachers and schools are given the freedom and creativity to prepare students without being overburdened by federal regulations. If such a compromise can be reached, it is possible that we might develop a structure that will make a positive difference in our schools. Whatever the future might hold, after considering Barack Obama's history and views, one cannot doubt that he cares deeply about improving schools and colleges. It is instructive that the money that he was awarded for the Nobel Peace Prize will be used "to help city kids get into college."[27]

Further proof of the president's commitment to education can be seen in a letter he wrote to his daughters during the early days of his administration. In this message, he wrote, "I want all our children to go to schools worthy of their potential—schools that challenge them, inspire them, and instill in them a sense of wonder about the world around them. I want them to have the chance to go to college—even if their parents aren't rich. And I want them to get good jobs: jobs that pay well and give them benefits like healthcare, jobs that let them spend time with their own kids and retire with dignity."[28]

To meet these lofty objectives, he, along with his critics, should heed the words of the man who has been called the father of the public schools. Over a century and a half ago, Horace Mann wrote, "Some eulogize our system of Popular Education, as though worthy to be universally admired and imitated. Others pronounce it circumscribed in its action, and feeble, even when it acts. Let us waste no time in composing this strife. If good, let us improve it; if bad, let us reform it."[29]

This is the dilemma we face as a nation, and its importance cannot be overestimated. As is frequently the case, it was Abraham Lincoln who said it best when he stated in an early campaign speech, "Upon the subject of education, not presuming to dictate any plan or system respecting it, I can only say that I view it as the most important subject which we as a people can be engaged in."[30] Whether another president from Illinois can meet the challenge articulated by Abraham Lincoln and Horace Mann remains to be seen.

NOTES

1. Dorie Turner, "Obama Promise: Brighter Education Futures for Kids," *Seattle Times*, 14 March 2010, seattletimes.nwsource.com/html/nationworld/2011341806_apusobamaeducation.html (accessed 15 March 2010).

2. Ibid.

3. Stephen Sawchuk, "Unions Object to Proposals on Teachers, Principals," *Education Week*, 26 March 2010, www.edweek.org/ew/articles/2010/03/26/27esea-teach.h29.html (accessed 26 March 2010).

4. Froma Harrop, "Obama Administration Shows Guts by Taking On Teachers," *Seattle Times*, 4 March 2010, seattletimes.nwsource.com/html/opinion/2011259468_harop05.html (accessed 5 March 2010).

5. Sam Dillon, "With Federal Stimulus Money Gone, Many Schools Face Budget Gaps," *New York Times*, 7 February 2010, www.nytimes.com/2010/02/08/education/08educ.html?ref=education (accessed 8 February 2010).

6. Terence Chea, "Schools Face Big Budget Holes as Stimulus Runs Out," *Washington Post*, 14 February 2010, www.washingtonpost.com/wp-dyn/content/article/2010/02/14/ar2010021401876.html (accessed 16 February 2010).

7. Alyson Klein, "275,000 School Jobs on Chopping Block, Survey Says," *Education Week*, 4 May 2010, www.edweek.org/ew/articles/2010/05/04/31jobs.h29.html (accessed 4 May 2010).

8. Nick Anderson, "Obama Administration Says It Supports Measure to Avoid Teacher Layoffs," *Washington Post*, 13 May 2010, www.washingtonpost.com/wp-dyn/content/article/2010/05/13/AR2010051305219.html (accessed 26 May 2010).

9. Thomas Hatch, "Four Flawed Assumptions of School Reform," *Education Week*, 4 December 2009, www.edweek.org/ew/articles/2009/12/09/14hatch.h29.html (accessed 8 December 2009).

10. Ibid.

11. Jim Taylor, "Education: Failing Students, Not Failing Schools," *Psychology Today*, 12 April 2010, www.psychologytoday.com/blog/the-power-prime/201004/education-failing-students-not-failing-schools (accessed 13 April 2010).

12. Ibid.

13. Clarence Page, "Today's Mom is Older, More Educated . . . and Single," *Daily News*, 11 May 2010, A4.

14. Ibid.

15. Valerie Strauss, "Goodlad on School Reform: Are We Ignoring Lessons of the Last 50 Years?" *Washington Post*, 27 April 2010, voices.washingtonpost.com/answer-sheet/john-goodlad/goodlad-straight-talk-about-ou.html (accessed 4 May 2010).

16. Valerie Strauss, "Deborah Meier's Education Advice to Obama," *Washington Post*, 4 May 2010, voices.washingtonpost.com/answer-sheet/deborah-meier/deborah-meiers-eduation-advice.html (accessed 4 May 2010).

17. Ibid.

18. Margaret Spellings, "School Accountability down the Rabbit Hole," *Dallas News*, 18 March 2010, www.dallasnews.com/sharedcontent/dws/dn/opinion/viewpoints/stories/DN-spellings_19edi.State.Edition1.26853a5.html (accessed 26 March 2010).

19. Wayne Au, "Obama, Where Art Thou? Hoping for Change in U.S. Education Policy," *Harvard Educational Review*, vol. 79, no. 2 (2009), 311.

20. Debra Viadero, "In Her Book, Ravitch Recants Long-Held Beliefs," *Education Week*, 4 March 2010, www.edweek.org/ew/articles/2010/03/04/24ravitch_ep.h29.html (accessed 12 March 2010).

21. Ibid.

22. Ibid.

23. Steve Inskeep, "Former 'No Child Left Behind' Advocate Turns Critic," *National Public Radio*, 2 March 2010, www.npr.org/templates/story.php?storyid=12409100 (accessed 2 March 2010).

24. Sam Dillon, "Scholar's School Reform U-Turn Shakes Up Debate," *New York Times*, 2 March 2010, www.nytimes.com/2010/03/03/education/03ravitch.html (accessed 3 March 2010).

25. Brad C. Phillips, "An Antidote to Ravitch Whiplash," *Education Week*, 16 March 2010, www.edweek.org/ew/articles/2010/03/17/25phillips.h29.html (accessed 17 March 2010).

26. Ibid.

27. Lindsey Christ, "Obama's Nobel Prize Money to Help City Kids Get into College," NY1.com, 2 April 2010, www.ny1.com/1-all-boroughs-news-content/top_stories/116328/obama-s-nobel-prize-money-to-help-city-kids-get-into-college (accessed 6 April 2010).

28. Donna Gundle-Krieg, "Barack Obama's Letter to His Daughters Emphasizes Education," *Blitz Krieg Publishing*, 19 January 2009, www.examiner. com/x-1393-Detroit-Education-Examiner~y2009m1d19-Barack-Obamas-letter-to -his-daughters-emphasizes-education (accessed 1 September 2009).

29. Joy Elmer Morgan, *Horace Mann: His Ideas and Ideals* (Washington, D.C.: The National Home Library Foundation, 1936), 49.

30. "Abraham Lincoln Quotes and Quotations," www.topicscites.com/abraham -lincoln/quotes.html (accessed 6 April 2010).

Index

About the Author

William Hayes has been a high school social studies teacher, department chair, assistant principal, and high school principal. From 1973 to 1994, he served as superintendent of schools for the Byron-Bergen Central School District, located eighteen miles west of Rochester, New York. During his career, he was an active member of the New York State Council of Superintendents and is the author of a council publication titled *The Superintendency: Thoughts for New Superintendents*, which is used to prepare new superintendents in New York State.

Mr. Hayes has also written a number of articles for various educational journals. After retiring from the superintendency, he served as chair of the Teacher Education Division at Roberts Wesleyan College in Rochester, New York, until 2003. He currently remains a full-time teacher at Roberts Wesleyan. During the past ten years he has written thirteen books, all published by Scarecrow Education and Rowman & Littlefield Education:

Real-Life Case Studies for School Administrators
Real-Life Case Studies for Teachers
Real-Life Case Studies for School Board Members
So You Want to Be a Superintendent?
So You Want to Be a School Board Member?
So You Want to Be a College Professor?
So You Want to Be a Principal?
Are We Still a Nation at Risk Two Decades Later?
Horace Mann's Vision of the Public Schools: Is It Still Relevant?

The Progressive Education Movement: Is It Still a Factor in Today's Schools?
All New Real-Life Case Studies for Administrators
All New Real-Life Case Studies for Teachers
No Child Left Behind: Past, Present, and Future

Breinigsville, PA USA
12 October 2010
247142BV00001B/4/P